THE

BUSINESS

OF

FAITH

Praise for The Business of Faith: How to Lead Yourself,
Unify Your Team, and Create a Remarkable Organization

In *The Business of Faith*, Matt and Jeff have penned a must-read road map to integrating the Christian faith into workplace leadership. Using poignant examples of their personal struggles to incorporate their faith at work, Matt and Jeff teach practical steps toward allowing Christ to be the Lord of our lives seven days a week. The scriptural principles in this book will help you become the leader Christ desires you to be—and also transform your company and its employees.

CLARK HUNT
Chairman and CEO, Kansas City Chiefs

Jeff and Matt have created a work that embraces what *Good to Great*'s Jim Collins calls, "the genius of the 'and." *The Business of Faith* is a well-crafted blend of leadership and theology. People today are not looking for work-life balance as much as they are looking for work-life integration. Drawing from sources as ancient as the book of Proverbs and as current as *Harvard Business Review,* Jeff and Matt have written the kind of book that you will not only give to aspiring leaders but also keep on your nightstand for reference, reassurance, and guidance. As they write, "Leaders changed by God change the world." Let God continue to change you through the pages of this book.

ERIC SWANSON
Missional Leadership Specialist, Leadership Network

After 20+ years as a leadership development consultant, I have read most of the books on the subject. What Matt Levy and Jeff Ward have done with *The Business of Faith* is unrivaled. There is no book on this topic with such balanced depth spiritually, strategically, and tactically. They've distilled true wisdom into an easy-to-digest format that will—if you choose to put it into practice—transform your life and your company.

JEFF SPADAFORA
Director of Global Coaching Services and Product Development, Halftime Institute

As the leader of an organization for the past decade, I wish I had read this much sooner in my life. Matt and Jeff lay out principles of leadership that will empower you to have a deep, meaningful impact in the lives of those you lead. An absolute must-read for leaders truly seeking to influence positive change within their organizations.

DAVID WILLIAMS
President, Williams Financial Group

One of the best leadership books I have ever read. *The Business of Faith* clearly connects biblical principles to daily, practical leadership in any environment. This book is a great roadmap to becoming the type of leader Jesus desires for you to be.

FRANK SCHUBERT
Principal, Expedition Capital

Matt Levy is one of the most innovative Christian business leaders in the country. The principles he and Jeff share will undoubtedly equip and empower leaders to grow and excel in their personal and professional lives. I highly recommend *The Business of Faith* and hope that these ideas will spread like wildfire throughout the business communities of the world.

JOE WHITE
President, Kanakuk Camps

The Business of Faith is a compelling and direct guide to best leadership practices, supported with personal application and the infinite wisdom of God's Word. This is a book that will equip you to improve your teamwork, guide your collective approach to leading your organization, and remind you of the greater purpose behind the blessing and responsibility of being in leadership.

BEN HEWETT
President, Austin Bridge & Road

Much more than a great read, *The Business of Faith* is an invitation to journey on the narrow path that leads to the greatest possible value: an abiding and transformational relationship with Jesus Christ that will change both your life and your leadership! No one can lead better than they follow, and this book shows why following Jesus is the best choice for you and all those you impact in business and in life. Choose well and do well!

CARLOS SEPULVEDA
Chairman of the Board, Triumph Bancorp, Inc., former President & CEO, Interstate Batteries

If you read this book and take its message to heart, you *will* be changed—and so will the organizations you lead. *The Business of Faith* is well worth the investment.

TED S. SCHWEINFURTH
Partner, Baker & McKenzie, LLP, Founder, Readers2Leaders

Most books written on leadership today tend toward the facile and formulaic: "Do this, don't do that, and *you* will succeed." Often, the emphasis is more on management science and *technique* rather than the essential character and virtues of the leader. Matt and Jeff rightly challenge that paradigm! They have penned a thoughtful and time-tested book of wisdom that should prove beneficial to any business leader, but especially to the one who is trying to follow Christ!

S. MICHAEL CRAVEN
President, BridgeBuilders

Jeff and Matt have gifted us with a book that pays attention to the *leader* in leadership. Leaders are not incidental to their leadership. Leaders are developed from the inside-out, even when the creative forces that drive this process are coming from the outside-in. These two able leader-authors have identified crucial intersections of this dynamic, and what they have to say about leadership is practical, insightful, instructional, and hopeful.

REGGIE MCNEAL
Missional Leadership Specialist, Leadership Network

Hold pen in hand as you read this book, because you will want to mark, check or underline strong points made on nearly every page. Levy and Ward capture truth that can only spring forth when timeless principle meets solid practicality, making *The Business of Faith* a surefooted pathway of professional and personal success.

BILL ROBERSON
President, Chase Couriers & Logistics, Inc.

I have often wished for a great discipleship book that is applicable to my life as a businessperson. Now I have it. I love how Matt and Jeff exemplify living purposefully in every aspect of their lives. *The Business of Faith* is an excellent catalyst for growth in godly leadership.

KYLE THOMPSON
Partner, Dale Gas Partners, Chairman/Partner,
Stronghold Energy Partners

We live in a celebrity-infatuated culture, where leaders of companies, countries, and churches are often put on glowing pedestals. Yet the most effective leader in the history of mankind, Jesus Christ, wasn't put on a pedestal, but on a cross. Jeff and Matt provide a wonderfully compelling look at effective servant leadership through the lens of Scripture, and their practical, winsome, Christ-centered approach will convict and challenge you. Lead on!

BRIAN FISHER
President, Human Coalition

Corporate America is in need of bold, servant leaders, now more than ever. In *The Business of Faith*, Jeff and Matt swim against the current of organizational and leadership expectations and clearly articulate how to be a successful business leader with a Christ-centered heart. If you want to positively change your professional relationships and the culture of your organization, this book is for you.

RUSS BROWN
Founder, Brown Fox, PLLC

A must read for anyone who desires to understand and execute vibrant leadership that helps those around them flourish. This book is a helpful, sincere, and pragmatic look at both the call and the exercise of Christ-centered leadership.

STEVE HARDIN
Dallas Campus Pastor, Village Church

Levy and Ward have written a refreshing book on the controversial topic of leadership. They provide practical and oftentimes personal leadership insights and principles to help you lead at *any* level, whether a small family business or a Fortune 500 company. This book is an excellent resource, and a reminder of how important the individual health of a leader is to any organization. Do yourself a favor: read this book and invest in yourself and in the future of your team.

KEVIN BATISTA
Missions Pastor, First Baptist Church Dallas

The Business of Faith explains the real source and power behind the key principles of humility, servant leadership, quality relationships, and team building found in Jim Collins' revolutionary *Good to Great*.

NEIL CURRAN
CEO, Biblical Communication International

THE
BUSINESS
OF
FAITH

How to Lead Yourself, Unify Your Team, and

Create a Remarkable Organization

MATT LEVY AND JEFF WARD

WITH D. R. JACOBSEN

Elevate Culture, Dallas, Texas

www.elevateculture.com

Companies, professional groups, clubs, and other organization may
qualify for special terms when ordering quantities of this title. For
information about sales promotions, group studies and educational
needs, contact Elevate Culture at info@elevateculture.com

ISBN: 0998214302

ISBN-13: 978-0998214306

Interior Design by Robin Black, Inspirio Design, LLC

Cover Design by Connie Gabbert, Connie Gabbert Design +
Illustration

Editing by Darla Hightower, DH Editorial Services

DEDICATION

*To Amy, Jonah, and Maggie, who God has used in ways
I never could have imagined to encourage, correct, love,
humble, and challenge me.
I love you deeply and love following Jesus with you.*
Matt

*To my wife, Kristie, who has patiently modeled
the value of loving and serving others well;
and my sons, Hayden and Hunter,
who forgive so easily, and lead me to my knees
(a great place for a leader to learn to follow).*
Jeff

TABLE OF CONTENTS

FOREWORD
Todd Wagner

I wish you were as fortunate as I am and *didn't need* to read this book.

Make no mistake, I have read it, and will again...but I didn't need to. That's because for years I have been blessed to live in close proximity to both Jeff and Matt—and their *lives* have been the book I have read and continually been challenged by.

Most of you will never have that benefit, so you must read this book. Matt and Jeff have done us all a great kindness in going through no small effort to share their life lessons and leadership insights in *The Business of Faith*.

Jeff and his wife, Kristie, are trusted partners with me here in Dallas, where we labor together to equip and empower others to lead. That means *serving* others, regardless of their life circumstance, in order to bring hope and opportunity throughout our community. Matt is the Cofounder and Managing Director of Credera, a highly respected consulting firm—and more importantly to me, a good friend. He and his wife, Amy, model for me what it means to be humble, to live life on purpose, and how to regain hope by allowing their mess to become their message.

It is my privilege to commend this book to you. Jeff and Matt understand what far too many business leaders and leadership books fail to see: *the best leaders must first lead themselves, and the most important job for leaders is to figure out who is going to lead them.*

The further our world drifts from the true north of objective truth, the more we need to hear from those who navigate by the revelation of Scripture and an abiding relationship with Jesus. It has never been more necessary.

What God's truth teaches us about how to live and how to lead will *always be* relevant, yet sadly it is rarely seen in leaders today. Jeff and Matt both demonstrate that being willing to be *led* is the path that sets you free to be the leader you want to be *and* the leader others want to follow. These men aren't theoreticians or so-called business gurus. They're practitioners. They've learned to lead by actually *leading*, and more importantly, they've learned to lead by faithfully following the greatest leader of all time.

If I had to summarize the best way to grow as a leader, I'd say something like this:

> **Step one:** learn from the best—and remember the best is a *person*, not the latest trendy philosophy.
>
> **Step two:** pay attention to people who are consistently doing step one, while excelling in their personal lives and particular fields.

I don't think I can point to better examples than Jeff and Matt. I've seen over the years that they are absolutely committed to mastering the art of self-leadership, so I know they can effectively encourage you as you lead yourself and others.

Most of you reading this may never get to spend a day with Jeff and Matt in Dallas, but the beauty of this book is you can spend as many hours as you need with them. Right here, right now, learning about God's good desire for you and those you lead.

It's a call to follow who you are meant to be and an investment you won't regret.

Follow on,
Todd Wagner
Dallas, Texas

FOREWORD
Rob Borrego

As CEO of Credera, I've had the privilege of working daily with Matt for more than a dozen years, and I know Jeff well from church. I was honored when they asked me to write this foreword, and because of what I know about their leadership and character, I anticipated an excellent book.

However, I asked them for some extra time, because I couldn't speak with integrity until I'd read every word. Fortunately, a recent trip to Maryland for my son's national lacrosse tournament gave me the perfect opportunity.

As I read, I found myself nodding when they talked about self-leadership, conflict resolution, fear, relationships, unity, generosity, mentoring, and most of all, abiding in Jesus. However, I wasn't nodding simply because I agreed with their wisdom. I do, wholeheartedly, but it went beyond that. What set this book apart from any previous leadership book I've read was the fact that each time they discussed a principle or scriptural truth, I could think of a specific time I'd seen them live that out, even when there was an easier or safer alternative.

Whether at church, in the boardroom, meeting with clients, spending time with their families, or serving in the wider community, I have seen Matt and Jeff in action across countless circumstances. And what I admire most is that they are consistently *on mission*. That means they are always looking for ways to pursue Jesus and to encourage others to do the same.

These men practice what they preach to an extraordinary degree. Unfortunately, there are too many Christians in the marketplace who think something like, "Once I leave church and go to my job, I've got to be a different person. That's just how my business works."

Although tempting to believe, that is a lie. We *can* connect our Sundays with our Mondays. Matt and Jeff demonstrate that this isn't just a *possibility*...it's how God is calling and empowering us to live and lead.

People like me don't usually have the privilege of writing the foreword to a book. I'm not a well-known pastor or a best-selling author. I'm certainly not famous! However, I can tell you with confidence that Matt and Jeff consistently *do* what they *say*—and more importantly, do what *God* says. Daily, weekly, yearly, through exciting times of growth and through lean seasons. If you want to be a better leader *and* a more effective follower of Christ, digesting this book is well worth your time. And your energy. Because leading the way God wants you to lead will take both.

If you're ready to discover what God has to teach you about the business of faith—and about how you can implement that on a daily basis—turn the page.

Rob Borrego
Dallas, Texas

Chapter One

THE JOURNEY BEGINS

Choosing the Narrow Road

Leadership in many organizations is fundamentally broken.

For example, what adjectives come to mind when you think of the CEO, the pastor, or the politician? There are exceptions, but many leaders have developed an unfortunate reputation by association as being selfish, corrupt, or immoral. Many of us have experienced leaders who trumpet greed masked as exceeding expectations, or boast about exploiting workers in the name of productivity, or even espouse sentiments like, "nobody likes being around poor people."[1] More and more leaders find it difficult to consistently live out a positive, people-first value system at work—and far too many no longer bother to try.

Understandably, it is easy to become discouraged. However, these types of leadership disappointments provide Christian leaders with an amazing opportunity.

Scripture makes it clear that God calls Christian leaders to a higher standard, both in what we say and do.[2] When we

---

1   Robert Frank, "Billionaire Casino King: 'Nobody Likes Being Around Poor People,' " *Inside Wealth*, CNBC, April 7, 2016, http://www.cnbc.com/2016/04/07/steve-wynn-nobody-likes-being-around-poor-people.html.

2   James 3:1–6.

model excellent leadership, we can make an incredible positive impact. But that leadership must begin in our relationship with Jesus, who is the true light.[3] When we walk with Christ, we shine brightly in the workplace—and the darker the room, the brighter the light shines. Christian leaders who *consistently* live out their faith at work look very different from other leaders.[4] Such biblical, Christ-centered leadership is the only way to repair our broken businesses, nonprofits, and governments.

We wrote this book as much for ourselves as for other Christian leaders. As we discuss in the following chapters, there have been seasons in our lives when we have struggled to live out the vital principles of biblical leadership. In our journey as leaders we have experienced times of inconsistency, unwillingness, and outright failure. Yet God gives leaders proven, biblical ideas that must move from our heads to our hearts, from sentiments to core convictions—because when that happens the transformation is powerful.

We aren't theoretical experts on business—we're practitioners. In our various fields—Matt as an entrepreneur, and Jeff as a former lawyer turned outreach pastor—we've learned through our personal mistakes and experiences. Our leadership is informed by scriptural truths, as well as best practices and principles gleaned from working with over 500 clients, our mentors, and observing other leaders who are doing it right.

Too often Christian leaders make the key mistake of thinking that mission or significance happens "later": after we make a certain amount of money; on the weekends when we serve at church; when we go on a "mission" trip; or when we retire and "finally" begin to influence others and live for a bigger vision.

---

3 John 1:9.
4 Matt. 5:14–16.

But the reality is that we can live lives of significance right now. We can lead our organizations and develop our people in our current position. We can lead out of a vibrant and thriving relationship with Christ today. Work is truly the primary means of loving our neighbors, serving our communities, and developing others—and being developed ourselves.

We are convinced that the following principles transform our personal leadership and the organizations we influence:

> *Effective conflict resolution yields greater influence.*
> *Fear is a leadership barrier that must be overcome.*
> *Relationships are the currency of work.*
> *Unity must be fought for and protected.*
> *Generosity is the best investment in any relationship.*
> *Mentorship and discipleship are the goals of biblical leadership.*

These principles may be easy to understand, but they are difficult to execute. Yet leaders who put these principles into practice are making a significant positive impact in their business for Christ.

Being an effective, healthy leader is a lifelong process, not a destination—and we are on this journey alongside you. In our culture, the church and the business world don't always work well together. Unfortunately, church and business leaders often believe something like, "If you let us do *our* thing, we'll let you do *your* thing." That attitude is fundamentally harmful, as we'll see throughout this book.

Rather, we believe Christian business leaders who want to follow Jesus with their whole lives must learn to apply biblical principles at work, in a way that consistently integrates faith and daily decisions.

This is what the Bible refers to as the narrow road: choosing what is right, even though it is more difficult, to reach a reward beyond value. "Enter by the narrow gate. For the gate is wide and the way is easy that leads to destruction, and those who enter by it are many. For the gate is narrow and the way is hard that leads to life, and those who find it are few" (Matt. 7:13–14).

Narrow-path options are offered to us every day, but they take more time, more courage, and require longer-term thinking. Wide-path options promise immediate comfort, pleasure, and recognition. We must ask ourselves daily, sometimes even hourly, "What is the narrow-path option?" And then we must pray, "Lord, help me make the narrow-path decision and walk it."

For example, narrow-path leaders faithfully pursue the "One Anothers" of Scripture: love one another, speak truth to one another, pray for one another, serve one another, encourage one another, and be available to one another.[5]

Can you imagine how your organization would be transformed if you walked out these principles every day?

It Starts with Us

Leaders, with few exceptions, get the organizations they deserve. The Bible speaks to this idea directly: "Can a fig tree, my brothers, bear olives, or a grapevine produce figs? Neither can a salt pond yield fresh water" (James 3:12).

> Many leaders expect to change their teams without first being willing to change themselves.

Leaders reproduce what they model. The way we speak, serve, handle conflict, overcome fear, build relationships,

---

5   See, for example, 1 John 4:11; Matt. 18:16; 1 Cor. 6:1–4; Prov. 12:19; Eph. 4:1–3; James 5:16; Phil. 2:3–4; Gal. 5:13; Mark 8:6–7; 1 Thess. 4:18; Acts 4:32. Credit to Todd Wagner for this list.

pursue unity, give generously, pour into the lives of others…how we lead is closely monitored and emulated by those on our teams. Many leaders expect to change their teams without first being willing to change themselves.

Consider a few questions. On a scale of 1 to 10:

1. How healthy am I professionally, emotionally, relationally, and spiritually?
2. How healthy would my team say I am?
3. How healthy is my team?
4. Now consider this: What if my health and my team's health are highly correlated? Jesus teaches that "a disciple is not above his teacher, but everyone when he is fully trained will be like his teacher" (Luke 6:40).

You have been appointed by God[6] as a steward, one who has responsibility for your team's growth during this season of their lives. It may be difficult to digest, but any change you desire to see in your organization must begin with you. When your team is fully trained, they will be like their teacher. When you are in the middle of working through an employee issue or dealing with financial pressure, long-term change may seem more like a daydream than reality.

The frustrations many feel in this area are normal. Progress can feel slow and sometimes seem nonexistent.

But it *is* worth the effort.

We've seen many leaders miss their opportunity here. They want a company or a team that's healthy, but unfortunately they are unable to admit their *team's* health mirrors their *own* health.

---

6   Rom. 13:1; John 15:16.

You and your team can be healthy—and you can do more good through your business than most people think possible.

To close this introduction, each of us is going to tell a personal story that provides some background on the topics of this book. We hope that our experiences will resonate and that you will choose to join us on this journey.

Matt's Story: A Difficult Choice

"Matt, I think you need to read this."

I looked up from our breakfast meeting to see one of my business partners handing me his iPad so I could read an email he had received from someone we both knew.

"It's feedback from a former employee. Unsolicited feedback. He says some pretty rough stuff about you."

As I scanned the pages of text, I felt the first spark of anger. My eyes picked out certain phrases.

Untrusting. Not Data Driven. Unwilling to Define Success. Perfectionistic.

The spark of anger had definitely caught fire, and flames were beginning to rise. My mind raced. *Who does he think he is?*

Suddenly, my thoughts halted. Somehow I understood I was facing a decision that would shape my personal and professional growth, as well as shape our company and the lives of our employees.

One path was easy, the other far more difficult.

It would be almost effortless to take the wide path and dismiss the feedback. I could discount it as coming from a former employee with limited perspective of our challenges. I could simply move on with my day. Some of the remarks would continue to sting, yes, but that was the sort of injury I could deal with. In fact, some well-chosen comments of my own would help to heal it. *Typical sour grapes...just reinforces that his departure was a good thing for the company.*

But what about the narrow and difficult path?

It would be doubly difficult. Of course the remarks would be hurtful to read in full. Worse than that, however, was the reality that reading them meant considering whether anything said was true of my leadership. Perhaps I was untrusting or perfectionistic...or worse. Perhaps such weaknesses were in fact a blind spot, and I'd been recklessly swerving in and out of lanes, unaware of the harm I was causing to others.

As I thought about the email, and as my feelings of anger and hurt threatened to lead me in the wrong direction, what would I choose? I forwarded the email to several friends, both inside and outside the company. By God's grace, my friends helped me choose the narrow, and more difficult, path.

Choosing the narrow path was far more painful, but also resulted in one of the most important seasons of growth in my life. I decided to read the feedback, to evaluate it, to allow others to inform my opinion of it, and to take it seriously—even though it would cost me potential relational capital, painful feelings, and worst of all, time. Yet that single decision led me into a rich season of growth as a leader and as a person. Growth that continues to bear significant fruit today. Looking back, I can't imagine what I would have missed out on, professionally or personally, had I chosen the wide and easy path.

Generally speaking, I credit the good decisions in my life to the Christian friends who have invested in me, both through our business and through our local church. At the time this happened, I had been part of both for several years, and my friends had spent time mentoring and discipling me. They were committed to helping me become a fully devoted follower of Jesus Christ in all areas of my life. My friends helped me understand that my ideas were less important than Jesus' ideas, since Jesus' ideas are consistently selfless and oriented toward others. My friends' investment in me has been transformative.

Although the word *disciple* doesn't often appear in business books, it's absolutely an essential business word. A disciple is someone who is a *learner*, someone who *chooses to follow and emulate a teacher.*

Make no mistake. We are all disciples and disciplers. We are influencing and being influenced by others every day. The question is: Who are we discipling? And who is discipling us? In business we may use different terms for the people who shape, guide, and challenge us—terms like hero or mentor—but the process we're describing is the same.

Those who invested in my life gave sacrificially of their time, energy, and resources. They wanted me to grow so I could help others. They wanted me to be healthy so our company could be healthier. And I believe God used my church—the community of people in my life who were following Christ—and my friends at work to mold me into the business leader that God was calling me to become. Throughout the process of personal change, it has been amazing to see how the teachings of Jesus inform the practices of business.

In business, examples of good practices include daily decisions, like taking a lower-level employee to an important lunch meeting, paying the IRS the correct amount, or asking for forgiveness when we have behaved or communicated poorly. Even though biblical truths inform our thoughts about business and are integrated into the way we practice business, the Bible makes it clear that doing good things does not save us. We are saved by grace through faith in Jesus Christ.[7] At the

---

7   Eph. 2:8–9.

same time, an active faith in Jesus results in a heart that wants to do good things and not just on Sundays![8] We are not simply talking about attending church or giving an offering—we are talking about business and the other six days.

Making such choices is part of our transformation as people and as leaders—and the most effective way to transform our businesses as well.

As a leader, choosing a path that requires us to be open to personal change—both as a leader and a human being—will be the hardest and best thing we ever do.

Our business culture does not have to remain the way it is today. We do not have to be a different person at home and at work.

One of the greatest revelations for me has been that God wants to grow me in order to use me and our business for His glory and for the good of His kingdom. In eternity *and* in the here and now.

Jeff's Story: A Change of Heart

For almost seven years of my life, I worked at a law firm headquartered in a seventy-two-story skyscraper that is one of the tallest buildings in the state. At the time I was a senior associate, on the cusp of partnership, and I enjoyed my job. What had drawn me to the practice of law—a sense of fairness and justice, the process of critical thinking and the judicial process, as a means to help people navigate difficult situations in life—continued to appeal to me. I was where I was meant to be…or so I thought.

Career-wise, I'd made it. I was checking off my profes-sional goals, one by one, just like I'd planned. I was locked in,

---

8   Eph. 2:10.

so to speak, and the next steps of my career seemed almost inevitable. Partner. Senior Partner. More prestige, more recognition, more responsibility, and more compensation to provide everything my wife and two boys ever needed.

When it came to winning at life, what else was there? I'll never forget the moment the answer to that question hit me: *there was a lot more.*

Late one evening, at a senior associate appreciation dinner, I was sitting at a table with six of my firm's partners and several other senior associates. I had won an award and an all-expense-paid vacation. I should have been riding high, but for some reason, my eyes began to scan the room. I looked at the people sitting around those tables, and suddenly I realized that I was previewing my future.

A nice guy at work, but divorced again and in the middle of a custody battle…single and working eighty hours a week…dealing with stress-related health problems…

And that was just the start of the list. On the outside I looked calm, but on the inside I felt a rising tension. *Odds are,* I realized, *if things didn't change, these stories will become my story. I probably won't be any different, even if I want to.*

It was hard to escape the conclusion that I wasn't headed in the right direction—and for what? I could no longer pretend that my future—longer hours, even with higher pay—had much to do with the reasons I'd become a lawyer. In fact, my future seemed to be taking me *away* from those reasons. Somewhere along the way, my original goal line had moved. And in that moment, I knew something needed to change.

Like the choice that Matt described earlier, I picked a new road that day.

For me, that choice meant leaving the only firm I'd ever worked for, and joining up with a few other colleagues to launch a new partnership and legal practice.

What I didn't realize was that *that* choice was merely the *beginning* of my journey. I had no inkling how God would use this new venture to renew my passion for evangelism and ignite a desire to explore how God could use my particular passion and skills in other ways, as well as to inspire me with some amazing glimpses of how God was already working around the world and in my city.

I worked in that new firm as a partner and owner for several more years. And I didn't have even the *hint* of a *clue* I'd eventually leave the legal profession entirely to serve full-time on a church staff—helping others to find their mission and deploy in kingdom service themselves.

One thing I've learned since that evening in the corporate dining room is that discipleship happens in the context of *business* as much as the context of church—or more. That will sound controversial, but it's true. Matt, in his story, shared the meaning of the word *disciple*: a learner who chooses to follow a leader. Think about where you spend most of your time, and about who you spend the greatest number of hours with. Assuming we work full-time, it's unrealistic to think church, or even family, has a bigger impact on us than work.

If you spend fifty hours a week at work, that's more than 40 percent of your waking hours. Do you spend fifty hours doing intentional things with your family? Do you spend even *five* hours at church or church events?

For many of us, work is the *primary* place where discipleship and transformation intersect—and that's absolutely *good* news.

Despite that reality, however, many leaders can believe work is morally neutral at best, a vehicle simply to generate income for others' ministry, or at worst, an amoral influence to be resisted. But it doesn't have to be that way! I know that for a fact, in part because of my friendship—and partnership—with my coauthor Matt, the managing director of a management and technology consulting firm. You probably haven't heard of it, because it doesn't have the public brand recognition of an AT&T or a Southwest Airlines. But what it does have is the recognition of two very important groups: its employees and the community.

Matt's company has consistently been ranked among *Texas Monthly*'s "Best Companies to Work for in Texas," as well as *Inc.*'s "5,000 Fastest Growing Private Companies in America."[9]

> For many of us, work is the *primary* place where discipleship and transformation intersect—and that's absolutely *good* news.

I know many of its employees personally, and they are living lives of purpose, integrity, and impact. It's the kind of business where you're encouraged to be the same person at work and at home, which helps create a culture of excellence and fulfillment. And let me tell you, if every business in our city was like their business, the city would be transformed.

Dallas has been called the "richest poor city in America." Its challenges are staggering, yet too many local leaders with vast resources—creativity, talent, financial resources, and so on—are running full-steam toward the wrong end zone. Other leaders are wondering if there are ways to deploy beyond a corporate "service day" or writing a check to a local charity. Many well-intentioned marketplace leaders know there is more than this—they just don't know where to start.

---

9 Over the last several years, our church has been ranked as one of the best places to work in Dallas by *The Dallas Morning News*. It is the only church on the list.

It's time to change that, beginning with a change in the leaders themselves.

The Real Story of Healthy Leadership

When we recall moments in our lives that have impacted us, they often hinge on story, Scripture, or song. These three gifts seem to have a unique power to influence and move us, which is why this book utilizes story and Scripture often, specifically for the purpose of planting truth in a way that will bear fruit. Scripture itself often uses story to teach us. That's how the people of Israel learned about God's character ("Remember the whole way that the LORD your God has led you these forty years in the wilderness."), worshipped in the Psalms ("The LORD is my shepherd."), and it's how Jesus spoke to people ("A farmer went out to sow his seed.").[10]

When even a simple sentence changes your life, isn't it true that you still construct a story about it? Imagine someone recounting a transformative moment. *I'll never forget the time I realized I needed to change course. I was on a red-eye from O'Hare to Heathrow, unable to sleep, and suddenly a line on my Kindle jumped out at me. I remember I had so much energy all of a sudden, and my mind raced for more than an hour, spinning out idea after idea in my head...*

So the more stories we share—mostly about our friends, colleagues, and history, along with key stories from the Bible—the more we hope you connect to the content in a way that is transformational. And before we transition to the next chapter, there's a final piece of our story we need to share. There's something else that unites us beyond our desire to grow healthy leaders and healthy organizations. It's Jesus.

---

10 Deut. 8:2; Ps. 23:1; Luke 8:5.

There's no other way to put it. We live in an area of the country where it remains relatively common to identify with Christianity and attend church on Sundays. In our experience, however, *few business leaders consciously live a life that fully integrates their faith and work, connecting Sunday to the rest of the week.*

We want to see that change. The principles and insights in this book have literally changed our lives. We are different leaders and husbands and parents and neighbors because on our best days we desperately depend on our daily relationship with Christ—what the Bible calls *abiding*—to live out these principles. We have seen God work through business leaders in powerful and inspiring ways, and it is our hope and our prayer that the principles in the following chapters will encourage and shape you, as they have us.

This isn't a book about information, but about *transformation*.

Your future isn't written yet—and your past does *not* need to determine your future. Every failure and false start can be used by God. Every bad decision can be redeemed. With God, nothing you've experienced needs to be wasted. God's grace can redeem your past and use it to bring about a better future, both for you and for those who are waiting to hear your story. God wants to use your story to bring hope to others. Your scars can be a source of hope and encouragement to others. God promises to redeem you, purify you, and make you zealous for the good works He has prepared for you. We see this in the Bible:

> For the grace of God has appeared, bringing
> salvation for all people, training us to renounce
> ungodliness and worldly passions, and to live
> self-controlled, upright, and godly lives in the
> present age, waiting for our blessed hope, the

appearing of the glory of our great God and Savior Jesus Christ, *who gave himself for us to redeem us from all lawlessness and to purify for himself a people for his own possession who are zealous for good works.* (Titus 2:11–14, *emphasis added*)

God always has a plan. And He never makes a promise unless He has a purpose behind it and a plan to carry it out.

We've both experienced being in a position of leadership, yet wanting to lead more effectively. In fact, that's exactly where we *still* are. We often think about how we can do better, but *doing* better only takes us so far. Lasting transformation requires us to *be* better, and *being* better requires change from the inside out.

We cannot be better on our own. We need God. And just as businesses don't "drift" into success, you don't drift into spiritual growth. There is no magic bullet. It takes discipline and time.

And it takes God's grace.

> We often think about how we can do better, but *doing* better only takes us so far. Lasting transformation requires us to *be* better, and *being* better requires change from the inside out.

Conventional wisdom suggests that faith is a purely personal matter, and has no place in a business environment. We couldn't disagree more strongly. We believe the most effective leaders "take Jesus to work." Not when it's convenient or safe. And not because it's good for business—even though it may be at times—but because the leader who follows Christ will create an environment where employees thrive. Where employees love coming to work, where they have a vision and are part of something bigger and more important than the "bottom line," where they are empowered to be all that God intended, and where excellence is demonstrated in every facet of the organization. Such a company is far more likely to be healthy when compared to its competitors—and you've probably noticed that healthy things tend to grow.

But we're getting ahead of ourselves. If what we've shared so far fundamentally goes against the grain of who you are, we'll understand if you pass this book on to someone else. After all, this book is narrowly focused on those few leaders who want to influence significant change, but who are willing to start with themselves—and these leaders know they need Jesus to do it.

Finally, it's important to note that throughout this book we plan to revisit the amazing, transformative love God has for each one of us. It is a love that caused God to take action on our behalf, so that we could experience grace and forgiveness. A deep and clear understanding of the foundational truth of God's love is a prerequisite to truly transformative, impactful leadership. This kind of love removes the temptation to focus on short-term behavior modification. We don't need a Band-Aid as much as we need heart surgery.

The intersection of personal transformation and business leadership is where we continue our journey in the next chapter.

Discussion Questions:

1. What do you want out of this study?

2. Scripture encourages us to examine ourselves and "remove the log from our eye" before we can be helpful to others. On a scale of 1 to 10:

   a. How healthy are you professionally, emotionally, relationally, and spiritually?

   b. How healthy would those you work most closely with say you are?

   c. How healthy is your team?

"Let a person examine himself." (1 Cor. 11:28)

"And see if there be any grievous way in me, and lead me in the way everlasting." (Ps. 139:24)

Chapter Two

THE LEADER

The Journey Begins Within

We know Steve Jobs as a visionary leader who grew Apple into one of the largest, most influential companies in the world.

Few of us remember, however, that early in his career he was ousted from his own company. In 1985, at the age of thirty, Jobs suffered what he called a "devastating" defeat when he was removed from a leadership position in the Macintosh division. Jobs and then-CEO John Sculley disagreed about the Mac, which Jobs championed. Though the revolutionary product got excellent reviews, it suffered disappointing sales. Jobs continued to fly a literal pirate flag over the building where the Mac division operated, determined not to budge an inch from his views. Apple's board of directors demoted Jobs, taking away his control of the Mac group.

Jobs was a famously demanding, hard-driving leader—so much so that he was unable to continue working alongside Sculley when their conflict escalated. The internal conflict tore the company apart. Apple wouldn't begin to truly recover for a decade.[11]

---

11 For more on the story, see Joel Siegel, "When Steve Jobs Got Fired by Apple," *ABC News*, Oct. 6, 2011, http://abcnews.go.com/

When the leadership of a company is fractured, the cracks deepen and spread throughout the organization. Corporate strength starts at the top, and no corporate asset—not strong financials, not admired products, not a history of success—is as important as the strength of its relationships.

Your effectiveness as a leader hinges on the quality of your relationships. And as a Christian leader, the quality of your relationships *correlates directly to what you believe*. If your leadership is not rooted in an abiding relationship with Jesus and the truth of His Word, you will not be able to establish the types of relationships your organization needs. Healthy organizations are characterized by team members who have high levels of trust and confidence in one another.

> Corporate strength starts at the top, and no corporate asset—not strong financials, not admired products, not a history of success—is as important as the strength of its relationships.

The self-leadership this requires is difficult, but God enables and empowers personal transformation. Why? Because God wants *your* work to be *His* work. And you can't do His work unless you know Him.

Leaders have been given the wrong message. They've been told that they need to *do* more in order to get better results— but this is only a half-truth. Yes, leaders need to do certain things, and do them well. But some of us need to focus more on *being* and less on *doing*.

It is *not* what you do on your own that determines your

Technology/steve-jobs-fire-company/story?id=14683754; and Graham Winfrey, "Why Steve Jobs Left Apple 30 Years Ago Today," *Inc.*, September 17, 2015, http://www.inc.com/graham-winfrey/why-steve-jobs-left-apple-30-years-ago-today.html.

effectiveness, but *who* you remain connected to. That's what Jesus tells His disciples in John 15:

> Abide in me, and I in you. As the branch cannot bear fruit by itself, unless it abides in the vine, neither can you, unless you abide in me. I am the vine; you are the branches. Whoever abides in me and I in him, he it is that bears much fruit, for apart from me you can do nothing. If anyone does not abide in me he is thrown away like a branch and withers; and the branches are gathered, thrown into the fire, and burned. If you abide in me, and my words abide in you, ask whatever you wish, and it will be done for you. By this my Father is glorified, that you bear much fruit and so prove to be my disciples. (John 15:4–8)

Notice the leadership truth Jesus highlights: the way to bear much fruit isn't to get out there and "make your own fruit," *but to abide in Jesus.* That is why lasting self-transformation happens when you encounter Jesus: since He loves you and wants you to bear fruit, Jesus will change you—first as a person, and then as a leader.

He will do this, regardless of your circumstances, which may seem wonderful at times and unbearable during other times. Circumstances don't necessarily reflect clarity of God's will: see Job and Joseph.[12] The steadfast love of God *never* ceases, regardless of your circumstances. If you are abiding in Jesus, then you are where God wants you to be, and your life will demonstrate it.

---

12 You can read about the life of Joseph in Genesis, chapters 37–50, and the life of Job in in the book of Job.

So begin by leading yourself toward Jesus. As you abide more deeply with Him, your subsequent choices and behavior will align more and more closely with the plans God has for you.

Your Team Reflects What You Value

One of the greatest second basemen of all time understood that organizational values must begin with a leader's personal values. In 1994, Ryne Sandberg told the Chicago Cubs he was retiring. Why? "I am certainly not the type of person who can ask the Cubs organization and the Chicago Cubs fans to pay my salary when I am not happy with my mental approach and my performance."[13]

That kind of honest leadership is noteworthy because it is uncommon. Many leaders fail to lead themselves with the same level of intentionality with which they lead their organizations.

However, leading yourself well is the essential prerequisite to leading a healthy organization. In the same way that heat always transfers through a physical system in a specific direction, meaningful *personal* change must occur before meaningful *organizational* change can occur.

Mary Barra understood this when she took the helm at General Motors in 2014.

> Her approach to changing the culture is highly un-GM-like. She hasn't launched a program or put out a 10-point plan; almost incredibly,

13 "Cubs History," http://chicago.cubs.mlb.com/chc/history/chc_feature_sandberg.jsp.

she hasn't formed a committee. Her approach is modest and audacious at the same time: She proposes to alter the mindset by behaving differently every day than any GM CEO has behaved in decades, and through her example and a CEO's influence, to change the way everyone else behaves every day. As she says, "Culture is how people behave."[14]

The CEO of GM—a multibillion-dollar company with a 100-plus year history and over 200,000 employees—believes that the primary way she can influence her company is by the way she *behaves*. She understands her daily behavior and character will have a positive effect on her entire company, just as she understands that *values are caught more than they are taught*.

We are convinced she is right. *Harvard Business Review* (HBR) calls this reality the "Return on Character."[15] The article reports the findings that "CEOs whose employees gave them high marks for character had an average return on assets (ROA) of 9.35% over a two-year period. That's nearly *five times as much as what those with low character ratings* had; their ROA averaged only 1.93%" (emphasis added).

---

14 Geoff Colvin, "Mary Barra's (Unexpected) Opportunity," *Fortune*, September 18, 2014, http://fortune.com/2014/09/18/mary-barra-general-motors/.

15 "Measuring the Return on Character," *Harvard Business Review*, April, 2015, https://hbr.org/2015/04/measuring-the-return-on-character.

How Leaders Scored

Employees rated their CEOs on four traits using a 100-point scale, where 100 meant the leader "always" displayed the trait. The top scroers ("virtuoso CEOs") surpassed the lowest ones ("self-focused CEOs") across the board.

Integrity

VIRTUOSO CEO — 87

SELF-FOCUSED CEO — 70

Responsibility

VIRTUOSO CEO — 91

SELF-FOCUSED CEO — 70

Forgiveness

VIRTUOSO CEO — 82

SELF-FOCUSED CEO — 70

Compassion

VIRTUOSO CEO — 87

SELF-FOCUSED CEO — 65

Showed trait half the time

SOURCE: KRW, from "Measuring the Return on Character," April 2015   ©HBR.ORG

Such bold findings were certainly a surprise. Interestingly, considering the measurable ROA for CEOs with high character ratings, the CEOs did a poor job at rating *their own character*. From the same study:

When asked to rate themselves on the four
moral principles, the self-focused CEOs gave
themselves much higher marks than their
employees did. (The CEOs who got high ratings from employees actually gave themselves
slightly lower scores—a sign of their humility
and further evidence of strong character.)

That is precisely why one of the more important steps
you can take as a growing leader is to commit to formal,
periodic reviews of how you lead.

- *Formal,* because casually asking others how you
  are doing as a leader won't provide the best data.
- *Periodic,* because becoming a better leader is an
  ongoing journey.

We make use of several leadership assessment tools and
are committed to taking the feedback seriously. (In appen-
dix A you will find the tool that Matt uses at his company.)
Such feedback has been an indispensable tool in our personal
growth as leaders, and we strongly encourage you to make
use of these.

In fact, you may wish to put this book down until you
have done so. Many of the topics we address in the following
chapters are predicated on an honest understanding of yourself. Several questions, for example, put leaders in a position
of vulnerability by asking for feedback from employees who
aren't typically provided a chance to speak so directly about
their boss's performance. Unfortunately, many leaders would
be tempted to avoid such feedback—and thus miss an opportunity for meaningful personal change.

As an example of the type of feedback we believe is vital to your growth, we've provided a few representative statements from one of the inventories.

Note that these statements invite those who work with the leader—from newly-hired twentysomethings to the board of directors—to participate in a review of the leader's *behavior*, not *intent*. If we're honest, we will admit that we are quick to judge *others* by their behavior and *ourselves* by our intent. Yet over time, our actions speak far more persuasively than our words, which is why we need our team to give us honest feedback.

How would those in your organization respond to the following statements about you? Each statement is marked on a scale from "Agree Strongly" to "Disagree Strongly."

- Gives encouragement to others
- Treats people with respect (i.e., like they are important people)
- Gives credit to those who deserve it
- Is able to forgive mistakes and not hold grudges
- Is someone people can trust
- Does not engage in backstabbing others (e.g., talking behind backs, etc.)
- Does not embarrass people or punish them in front of others
- Is sensitive to the implications of their decisions on other departments
- Is a fair and consistent leader and leads by example

These statements allow others in the organization (including direct reports) to provide feedback to the leader. There is a high likelihood the leader will discover blind spots and growth areas. For example, a leader may be continuing to grow revenue, yet be unaware of the negative long-term impact that withholding encouragement is having on the team.

A 360-degree review is not an original idea,[16] but it is extremely useful. When the process is administered well, the results have been helpful personally and with the leaders we have worked with.

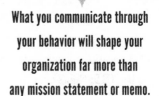

What you communicate through your behavior will shape your organization far more than any mission statement or memo.

Remember, what you communicate through your behavior will shape your organization far more than any mission statement or memo. The more honest you are with yourself, and the more willing *you* are to change, the more you can influence change in your organization.

Well, *Now* What?

Your willingness to be completely honest about your leadership is an important step on the journey. Understanding and dealing with reality is what healthy people and healthy organizations do. Unhealthy people avoid living fact-based lives. Instead, they live by their own distorted version of reality, and it affects every decision they make and every relationship they have.

However, when you deal with the facts about yourself, and your team sees you responding to that feedback, you will build trust and influence positive change in your organization.

Consider the case of Adrian Hanauer, the former general manager and current co-owner of the Seattle Sounders, one of Major League Soccer's most successful and well-attended

---

16 See, for example, James Hunter's books at http://www.jameshunter.com/books.htm.

teams.[17] Hanauer, by all accounts, performed ably as GM, but stated publicly that the GM role wasn't the best place for him to optimally contribute to the needs of the organization. In the 2014 off-season, the Sounders pulled off a major coup as Hanauer *acted* on his *words*, finding a way to optimize the GM role and replace himself.

"I always said that if the best General Manager was available, I would hire that person to replace me," said Hanauer. And in 2015, that's exactly what Hanauer did. He hired Garth Lagerwey, the former GM of Soccer Operations for the Real Salt Lake organization, as the Sounders new GM. Widely regarded as one of the top GMs in the league during his seven seasons in Utah, Lagerwey oversaw a team that perennially reached the playoffs and won a championship.[18]

We believe that Hanauer's ruthless examination of his leadership and the associated facts is exactly what is required of healthy, effective leaders.

Be honest: Would you hire your own replacement? When asked what he looks for in a prospective employee, Facebook's founder, Mark Zuckerberg, said, "I will only hire someone to work directly for me if I would work for that person."[19]

When you see rising talent in your firm, do you feel threatened or spurred on to a higher degree of excellence? What if that rising talent is your direct report?

---

17 See data at "Seattle Sounders FC," *Wikipedia*, http://en.wikipedia. org/wiki/Seattle_Sounders_FC.

18 "Sounders FC Appoints Garth Lagerwey as General Manager and President of Soccer," January 6, 2015, http://www.soundersfc.com/ post/2015/01/06/sounders-fc-appoints-garth-lagerwey-general-man- ager-and-president-soccer.

19 Geoff Weiss, "Mark Zuckerberg: I Would Only Hire Someone to Work for Me If I Would Work for Them," *Entrepreneur*, March 5, 2015, http://www.entrepreneur.com/article/243660.

When leaders periodically choose to be evaluated by those they lead—*and then act on that information*—they increase relationship capital. That capital can then be spent to make important changes in the organization…changes the organization is likely to unite behind.

This paradoxical idea of ruthless self-honesty by leaders is captured in a portion of Jim Collins' well-known "levels of leadership," summarized here by the *Harvard Business Review*:

> One final, yet compelling, note on our findings about Level 5: Because Level 5 leaders have ambition not for themselves but for their companies, they routinely select superb successors. Level 5 leaders want to see their companies become even more successful in the next generation and are comfortable with the idea that most people won't even know that the roots of that success trace back to them. As one Level 5 CEO said, "I want to look from my porch, see the company as one of the great companies in the world someday, and be able to say, 'I used to work there.'" By contrast, Level 4 leaders often fail to set up the company for enduring success. After all, what better testament to your own personal greatness than that the place falls apart after you leave?[20]

What do you want your legacy as a leader to be?

---

20 Jim Collins, "Level 5 Leadership: The Triumph of Humility and Fierce Resolve," *Harvard Business Review*, July–August, 2005, https://hbr.org/2005/07/level-5-leadership-the-triumph-of-humility-and-fierce-resolve.

Self-leadership is difficult, but the most rewarding times in our lives are often preceded or precipitated by a trial. Even apart from professional insights and growth, the richness of abiding with Christ during the trial is, in itself, a reward.

Truly, it is only through our abiding relationship with Jesus that we can move toward such honesty in the first place. The world expects leaders to protect and insulate themselves, but followers of Jesus need never be limited by such false dreams of safety and self-preservation.

Don't Run from Greatness

The desire you have to be a great leader is not wrong.

The skills you use every day to lead your organization are gifts from God, given to you, specifically, for a reason. You see, when God created you, He was intimately involved in every step of the process (Ps. 139). And this might surprise you, but even before you were born, God had a mission for you to accomplish (Eph. 2:10).

Consider a parable Jesus told in Matthew 25. A man was going on a journey, but before he left he gave three of his servants some money: five bags of gold for one, two bags for another, and a single bag for the third. Once the master left, the first two servants put the money to work, while the third hid his in a safe place. When the master returned, he asked for a report. The first two servants told the master that they were able to double his money by putting it to work, while the third reported that he simply locked the bag of gold away for safekeeping. Predictably, the master was pleased with the first two servants, praising them and letting them know that because they were faithful, they will be given even more responsibility in the future. He also invited them to share in his success.

Less predictably, however, the master was *angry* with the third servant.

Though the servant has lost none of his master's money, the master nevertheless called him wicked and lazy. Jesus was using the bags of gold to represent the gifts God gives us. God plans to accomplish great good in the world through ordinary people like us—especially through our work. Because of his fear, however, the third servant buried the gifts God had given him, *and buried gifts represent missed opportunities to accomplish God's purposes in the world.*

If you're reading this, we believe there is a good chance you are the first or the second servant in Jesus' parable. Not only have you been granted a wide array of good gifts, but God expects you to actively use, invest, and multiply those gifts, for the sake of His kingdom and purposes.

In Mark 10, James and John approached Jesus with a seemingly strange request. Each wants to be given the highest place of glory in heaven, seated at the right hand of Jesus.

Jesus responded with a reality check, asking if they have the faintest idea what they are really requesting. Can they endure the same things He is about to suffer?

James and John were undeterred. "We can," they answer.

Jesus replied that they *will* suffer in the same way, but that such heavenly rewards are not for Him to grant. "Those places belong," He said, "to those for whom they have been prepared."[21]

Now notice what Jesus *doesn't* say.

He doesn't scold James and John for asking to be great. He doesn't reprimand them for having the wrong priorities. He doesn't tell them that they would not receive a great reward in heaven.

---

21 Mark 10:34–40.

Quite the opposite, in fact. *Given the desire of James and John to be great, Jesus makes sure that they know the stakes and the requirements.*

The brothers had been aspiring to positional authority and greatness, as evidenced by sitting in a special place next to Jesus in eternity. Jesus helped them understand the rulers of their present day had positional authority, but that His disciples ought to be seeking something *even greater.* This is reinforced in another conversation Jesus had with His disciples about the subject:

> An argument arose among them as to which of them was the greatest. But Jesus, knowing the reasoning of their hearts, took a child and put him by his side and said to them, "Whoever receives this child in my name receives me, and whoever receives me receives him who sent me. For he who is least among you all is the one who is great." (Luke 9:46–48)

In that culture, children were at the lowest level of societal importance, whereas the male religious leaders were arguably at the highest level. Jesus was letting His disciples know that He was changing the goal when it came to greatness— so much so that those who the culture derided as worthless or insignificant would actually be elevated to places of honor in God's kingdom. In God's economy, whoever wants to be great must become a servant, and whoever wants to be honored must become a servant to all.

Jesus is not telling us that no one will be great. Rather, He is telling us *how* to be great. He redefines how we are to understand greatness, and makes sure we count the cost before we pursue it.

So don't run from greatness. Don't pretend that you don't desire it. There's no need to put up a front of false humility and publicly pretend that you don't *really* want to *crush it* at work and in life.

Rather, follow the example of Jesus, the greatest leader who ever lived. He set the standard for true greatness by serving and by laying down His life for us. When you walk in that type of greatness it will transform your character *and* your organization.

We Are All Theologians

We Christian leaders, perhaps more than anyone else, must continually remind ourselves of the truth that it is God, not our culture, who provides the measurement of our greatness and success. In many ways, we will be exploring the nuances of that truth throughout this book. We can be taught certain skills and techniques, and learn to use them well, but no skills or techniques can take the place of an ongoing, abiding relationship with Jesus.

> What we believe about God drives our actions—whether we are aware of that influence or not.

As we mentioned at the start of this chapter, what you believe correlates to the quality of your relationships. And the truth is that *all* of us are theologians. What we believe about God drives our actions—whether we are aware of that influence or not. What we prioritize, the relationships we invest in, the way we spend our money...all of that hinges on what we believe about God, which is our theology.

And your theology has a dramatic impact on your health and effectiveness as a leader.

A friend of ours—let's call her "Rachel"—recently reminded us of this in an unforgettable way. Rachel is the principal of an urban high school for high-risk students. These are kids

who have been kicked out of other public schools or who are
reentering the classroom after spending time in juvenile deten-
tion facilities. It's an incredibly difficult job. Rachel has been
ignored, threatened, cussed out, and even shot at, and through
it all she keeps her focus on what is best for the kids.

Jeff went to visit her campus recently, and she described
a heartbreaking litany of challenges that these kids are facing: gang intimidation, violence, early sexual activity, teen
pregnancy, STDs, rampant drug use, a lack of opportunity, a
dearth of role models, and limited or no parental involvement,
to name only a few. The kids seemed trapped in a cycle of
hopelessness.

"I want to show you something," she said at one point,
unfurling a roll of butcher paper on a table. The paper was cov-
ered with phrases and short sentences, each written by a different hand. "Today I asked the kids an interesting question."

"And that was…?"

"I asked them who they thought God was."

Looking at the paper through that lens, the phrases began
to make a lot more sense.

The great pimp in the sky.

Old man upstairs.

Watching like a 'copter.

Such ideas, regardless of how the kids arrived at them,
couldn't help but change the way they act. They were negative
theological statements. A pimp uses and abuses you for his
own purposes, then discards you when you're of no further
use. If that was your view of God, how would it influence
your choices?

Rachel summed it up. "And we wonder why these kids are
involved in the things they're involved in!"

Whether you are an at-risk kid writing about God on

butcher paper, or the CEO of a successful company you built with your own hands, you are a theologian, and theology drives your behavior.

The most important thing about *us* is what we think about *God*.

That is why we cannot overstate the importance of a leader's abiding relationship with Jesus. Day in and day out, through all the ups and downs of business and family, a leader must remain connected to Jesus. Remember John 15? "Apart from me," Jesus said, "you can do nothing. If anyone does not abide in me he is thrown away like a branch and withers."

Sometimes that constant reliance can seem so small as to be trifling—but it isn't. On your way to an important meeting, what would happen if you popped into an empty conference room or hallway, found thirty seconds of silence, and prayed? "Father, I'm worried about the outcome of this meeting, but I don't need to worry about your love. Thank you for always loving me, and forgiving me, and promising to be with me. I need you in this meeting, and I know that you will be there. Help me to be quick to listen, slow to speak, and slow to become angry. Help me be a Proverbs 2 and a Colossians 3:12–17 leader. Help me ask great questions. Thank you, God, in the name of Jesus. Amen."

That's abiding! Remember, we must be intentional about remaining in Jesus for a reason: because we want to bear fruit. The fruit of the Spirit, Paul tells us in Galatians 5, is love, joy, peace, patience, kindness, goodness, faithfulness, gentleness, and self-control. We desire fruitful lives at work, at home, in our communities. In all that we do, we desire that our lives bear godly fruit, for the sake of the world.

Could your organization use more of that fruit? Let this verse encourage you as a leader and as a follower of Jesus:

[Jesus said,] "Truly, truly, I say to you, who-
ever believes in me will also do the works that
I do; *and greater works than these will he do.*"
(John 14:12, *emphasis added*)

Choosing the Hill Country[22]

Having escaped the Pharaoh's slavery in Egypt, the Israelites stood at the edge of something great. Behind them,
the Desert of Paran. Ahead of them, Canaan, the Promised
Land—literally, because God had promised it to them.

At God's command, Moses sent a leader from each of
the twelve tribes, and each man was tasked with exploring
Canaan and reporting back. What was the terrain like? How
many inhabitants were scattered across it, and how fierce
would the resistance be? Were there towns or fortified cities?
What about the farmland and pastureland?

These were the thoughts that ran through Moses's mind.
God had promised him that the Israelites would inhabit that
land, but that promise hadn't come with any specifics for the
moment. God trusted Moses, His chosen leader, to be part of
the plan. Finally, almost as an afterthought, Moses added a
command. "Bring back some fruit of the land."

Marching orders received, the twelve scouts split up and
infiltrated Canaan, including a man named Caleb, of the
tribe of Judah.

Forty days later, the scouts reported back to Moses, and
they delivered the good news first—probably because the "fruit
of the land" Moses requested is so tantalizing. It's pomegran-
ates and figs, along with a bunch of grapes so large that two of
the spies are carrying it together, hanging from a pole between

---

22 The following section is drawn from Numbers 13–14 and Joshua 14.

them. All the men agree that Canaan is a land perfect for cattle and crops and new communities where the Israelites can flourish—a land flowing with milk and honey.

But then comes the bad news: if the Israelites try to take the land by force, then the Israelite fighting men will be *crushed* like grapes by the local fighters. "We felt like grasshoppers compared to those guys," complain the scouts, "and they probably thought we *were* grasshoppers!" There seemed to be agreement that God messed up somehow when He promised Canaan to them.

Except Caleb, the lionhearted scout from the tribe of Judah, was having none of that. He silenced the crowd, and then spoke, telling everyone that the other scouts are wrong—they *can* take possession of Canaan. And they *should*.

He's simple and decisive. And he never said it would be *easy*—that's a theme we'll encounter over and over. There were walled cities and countless fighters to overcome. Nevertheless, he was confident, because God had promised.

What happened next is the opposite of a fairy-tale ending. The other scouts spread fear, uncertainty, and doubt (what many call FUD) among all the Israelites. The people lost the will to move forward. And God provided a fitting punishment for their lack of trust: for forty years, corresponding to the forty days spent scouting, the Israelites will wander the desert, rather than entering the Promised Land.

Now fast-forward in the story to the end of that desert exile. God has given His people another chance, and this time, led by Joshua, they successfully began to march into the Promised Land. The campaign opened with the famous battle of Jericho, where God proved beyond a shadow of a doubt the lesson that an earlier generation failed to learn: that it is through *God's power*, rather than force of arms, that the promise would be secured.

And as the Israelites continued their campaign, and the time came for the Promised Land to be fully conquered and shared among the twelve tribes of Israel, something stunning happened.

An aging warrior named Caleb—the same man who had been one of the original scouts—is still burning with passion. "I'm still standing here today, at the age of eighty-five," he said. "I'm as capable now as I ever was in my youth. Maybe more so!"

Then he gave a bit of a history lesson. He recalled the cowardice of the other scouts, forty-some years earlier, as well as the conviction that led *him* to follow God wholeheartedly. Then he quoted the promise of Moses, "The land on which your feet have walked will be your inheritance and that of your children forever, because you have followed the Lord my God wholeheartedly."

Caleb is looking forward to a well-deserved inheritance—and considering his past, surely he should receive the greenest of the green valleys. After all, when the other scouts were fearful, and turned their back on God's promise, and spread dissention, Caleb declared that he trusted God to deliver. Returning to Canaan so many years later, a leader such as Caleb should be allowed to enjoy the fruit of his faith, and take possession of the richest, choicest tracts of land.

Yet Caleb is not done recalling the promises of the past. "All of you heard the report, long ago, that this hill country contained some of the stoutest warriors, the most heavily-fortified cities, and the harshest terrain. It still does—and with God helping me, I will conquer it. Now give me this hill country that God promised to me."

Incredible. Caleb chose not to relax and rest in the green pastures, but to finish what God had started long before. He chose the hill country, where his enemies were still holed up, because he trusted God to deliver on His promises. What a picture of steady, persevering faith. Caleb kept his eyes fixed on the task God had given him, knowing that he could only be the *leader* God wanted him to be if he was the *person* God wanted him to be. And it should come as no surprise that Caleb's choice served as an example to the rest of the Israelites.

As we close this chapter, listen to the final line in Caleb's story, a line that is heartbreaking for its beauty and wisdom.

"Then the land had rest from war."

The faithful, consistent, difficult work you're doing to follow Christ more fully—to become a better person and a better leader—*is for a reason.*

Sometimes God gives us either/or choices. "Choose this day whom you will serve," said Joshua 24:14–15. "No one can serve two masters," said Jesus in Matthew 6:24.

There are other times, however, when God provides us with a both/and.

Abiding in Christ is good for you, and *good for your organization.*

When you, like Caleb, choose to follow God with "a long obedience in the same direction,"[23] your efforts *will* bear fruit. Caleb chose the hill country because he chose to follow God with his whole heart. And then the land had rest from war. It wasn't up to Caleb to *succeed*—that was God's job—but it was up to Caleb to honestly pursue faithfulness.

That's what leaders do. And then they watch the fruit grow.

---

23 From the title to Eugene Peterson's seminal book *A Long Obedience in the Same Direction: Discipleship in an Instant Society.*

Discussion Questions:

1. It is *not* what you do on your own that determines your effectiveness. What is your response to that biblical truth?

2. Is it true of your organization that values are "caught" more than they are "taught"?

3. Have you ever participated in a formal review of your leadership? If not, do you plan to?

4. What do you want your legacy as a leader to be?

5. Do you want to be a great leader? How will you demonstrate you are willing to allow Jesus to define greatness in your life?

Jesus called them to him and said to them,
"You know that those who are considered rulers of the
Gentiles lord it over them, and their great ones exercise
authority over them. But it shall not be so among you.
But whoever would be great among you must be your

servant, and whoever would be first among you must be slave of all. For even the Son of Man came not to be served but to serve, and to give his life as a ransom for many."
(Mark 10:42–45)

CONFLICT RESOLUTION

The Journey Toward Each Other

The quality of your relationships will largely determine your effectiveness as a leader. Normal relationships experience conflict. So it's crucial you understand how to work through difficult issues. Not avoid them, but *resolve* them. If you don't, individual instances of *unresolved* conflict will accumulate, fester, and ultimately ruin your team and organization.

Unresolved conflict is similar to a wall being built, one brick at a time. It is too easy for ongoing conflict to create real relationship barriers between team members. Sometimes these walls are low, and merely cause an inconvenience when stepped over. Projects take longer. Team members spend less time together. Certain people only enjoy working with certain people. Work is still accomplished, but at a slower pace because of the barriers.

Other times, however, unresolved conflict creates walls that are too high and thick to see or hear through. These walls prevent organizational goals from being achieved. Partnerships dissolve. Clients become former clients. Team members avoid each other.

Fortunately, *biblical* conflict resolution dismantles seemingly impenetrable walls. Brick by brick, section by section, conflict resolution breaks down barriers. And surprisingly, something else happens: in place of walls, bridges of trust are constructed.

"Blessed are the peacemakers," Jesus said in Matthew 5:9, "for they shall be called sons of God." God values peace, but it isn't automatic or inevitable. Enduring, complete peace—called *shalom* in the Bible—is something we must pursue and work toward. Sometimes we confuse peace with the absence of conflict. Yet there is a massive difference between peacemaking and peace *faking.* Sitting quietly behind a wall and doing your own thing is not peace, and neither is sticking your head in the sand when there is conflict on your team. The Christian leader must tear down walls, build trust, and love people in the process. The only way to do that is to abide in Christ and apply His principles.

> Every conflict is an opportunity to grow a healthier team and a healthier you.

Sometimes we believe that forgiveness has its limits, but Jesus shatters this paradigm in Matthew 18:21–22: "Then Peter came up and said to him, 'Lord, how often will my brother sin against me, and I forgive him? As many as seven times?' Jesus said to him, 'I do not say to you seven times, but seventy-seven times.'"

It's true that conflict resolution can seem like an inefficient way for leaders to spend their time. Real conflict resolution is rarely easy or quick. It is usually the opposite. Nevertheless, it is one of the most important skills for leaders to develop.

There are two ways to grow a plant. In one approach, a gardener may apply skill and wisdom to a variety of external circumstances, combined with the right amount of *time*. The gardener's objective is to yield the healthiest possible crop.

In a second approach, a gardener may decide the size of the crop is more important than its nutritional value, and heavily leverage pesticides and fertilizers. Both methods can produce large, healthy-looking plants, and yet both methods produce entirely *different* results. Results are about more than simply outward appearance. They are about who we are—and who we *become*—in the process, and this is especially true when it comes to conflict resolution.

Every conflict is an opportunity to grow a healthier team and a healthier you. Shortcutting the process will produce only artificial, short-term results.

And resolving conflict biblically begins with you.

Coworker Competition

We are convinced that effectively resolving conflict is one of the most important leadership skills we can bring to our organizations. Conflict begins when a person doesn't get what he or she wants or expects. That happens often in life. And even though we know conflict is inevitable, many leaders are hesitant, ill-equipped, or unwilling to deal with it. Leaders lack competency in this area because of its subjective nature and the painful process required to do it well.

To illustrate this, Matt has a story[24] about how conflict nearly tore his company apart. Embracing conflict helped him and his organization flourish in a way it never could have without it.

◆

---

24 Matt first told this story on his company blog. You can read more at https: //blog.credera.com/management-consulting/ conflict-at-credera-part-1-conflict-is-opportunity/.

Strange as it sounds, one of my most valuable relationships was born in the crucible of serious conflict.

The conflict first erupted between Rob and me during a time of leadership transition. Rob was our newly appointed CEO, and I was continuing to operate in the business as a founder. We knew the internal battles between founders and CEOs were all too common in the business world, but we believed our story would be different.

Unfortunately it wasn't. You could almost hear the echoing voice of the arena announcer: *Aaaand in this corner…* We were ready to rumble! During our first project together, a conflict began to surface. At the time, we were working at a client's office on their technology strategy. The two of us, along with three other members of our team, worked on the project for twelve consecutive weeks. We traveled to six cities together, developed a common understanding of the client's challenges, and generated actionable strategies and a multi-year delivery plan. It was an intense project that required us to spend a great deal of time together.

At the end of week four, Rob was leading a whiteboard session, sketching out his initial thoughts. I immediately responded with my own opinions, which would have required Rob to edit much of what he'd already added to the board. That was a moment of decision, though neither of us understood it at the time. We could have applied Proverbs 2 and sought to understand one another. We could have asked the other team members for input. We could have agreed to come back to the discussion after some time had passed.

Instead, we locked horns. It didn't really matter who was right, but both of us *believed* it mattered. Consequently, we became focused on *proving* our own point of view. Our weapons were many: rhetoric, persuasion, vocal tone, raised eyebrows, and other nonverbal cues. The tension was palpable. I'm sure our other team members felt it. The way we were proceeding, only *one* of us could "win." We'd managed to transform a brainstorming session into a zero-sum game.

It was the sort of discussion that friends can have and recover from—but Rob and I weren't friends yet. We were something much more dangerous: two leaders with strong opinions, strong personalities, and a lack of trust in each other. We had agreed to work together, but for both of us that still meant something closer to "giving orders" than being partners. It would have been better to actually seek to *understand* and *serve* each other.

If our nascent partnership was to grow, what we needed was the ability to work through conflict in a healthy way. But we weren't there yet.

Outside Perspective

In a recent survey[25] an astounding 43 percent of CEOs rated "conflict management skills" as the *number one target* for personal growth. Anecdotally, the report revealed that "most things that come to your desk only get there because there is a difficult decision to be made—which often has some level of conflict associated with it."

Nearly 100 percent of the CEOs in the survey reported that they desired to receive leadership advice and/or coaching from an outside source. However, *more than 60 percent do not receive any independent guidance.* Despite so many leaders

---

25 Center for Leadership Development and Research (CLDR) at Stanford Graduate School of Business, Stanford University's Rock Center for Corporate Governance, and The Miles Group. *Insights by Stanford Business,* "David Larcker: 'Lonely at the Top' Resonates for Most CEOs," July 31, 2013, http://www.gsb.stanford.edu/insights/david-larcker-lonely-top-resonates-most-ceos.

wanting to become better at resolving conflict, the majority are not receiving help. Stephen Miles, one of the study's authors and CEO of The Miles Group, summarizes the issue this way:

> Given how vitally important it is for the CEO to be getting the best possible counsel…to maintain the health of the corporation, it's concerning that so many of them are "going it alone." Even the best-of-the-best CEOs have their blind spots and can dramatically improve their performance with an outside perspective weighing in.

Such independent counsel is vital, especially when conflict reaches an impasse. Let's continue Matt's story.

◆

When Rob and I were struggling to resolve our conflict, we invited a mutual friend, Kyle, to join our board of directors. Both of us trusted Kyle and we knew he wouldn't "take sides." Rather, he would seek to do the right thing, morally and relationally, both for our friendship and for the organization.

When asked to help with a particular impasse, Kyle would say something like, "Let's park the current issue for a few minutes and work on the relationship. What are the relational or professional trust issues we need to discuss?"

Then Rob and I would take our focus off the impasse, instead communicating about macro-issues that were continuing to impede us.

> *When it seems like Matt is trying to take back his previous role, I feel like my authority is being undermined.*

> *When it seems like Rob is in command-and-control mode, I don't feel like his business partner or a fellow board member.*

Kyle helped us pay attention to the places where the relationship was damaged. He asked both Rob and me to "own" our part in the conflict and seek forgiveness from the other. This approach allowed us to begin the discussion by seeking to understand one another's *intent*, which was often misunderstood.

When those involved in conflict are willing to approach the relationship with understanding and grace, the impossible becomes possible. One key value of Kyle's involvement was his consistent counsel that Rob and I start working on our conflict by "looking in the mirror" and working on ourselves. It was only when I began with my own issues and responsibility that there was any improvement in the relationship.

Jesus said it best:

> Why do you see the speck that is in your brother's eye, but do not notice the log that is in your own eye? . . . You hypocrite, first take the log out of your own eye, and then you will see clearly to take the speck out of your brother's eye. (Matt. 7:3–5)

A conflict may be entirely our fault and we might not know it. Even if it feels like the other person is at fault, it is possible we have a blind spot and don't realize we are the reason a conflict exists.

We judge ourselves by our intent and others by their actions. Shouldn't it be the other way around?

Jesus is very clear that before we ask others to deal with the speck in their eyes, we must be willing to deal with the log in our own eye. As long as we have an obstruction blocking our vision, we will be unable to see how to help others.

What to Look for in External Advisors

Choosing the right external advisor for your situation is critical to the success of your organization and your personal growth. Elite athletes hire personal coaches who understand their strengths and weaknesses and work patiently to help them improve. Transformational leaders need the same thing.

Why would we believe it is a good idea to attempt this alone? Isolationist thinking doesn't make any logical sense and, not coincidentally, it is inconsistent with Scripture. Proverbs 18:1 says, "Whoever isolates himself seeks his own desire; he breaks out against all sound judgment."

When selecting an external advisor, find someone with a reputation for integrity, an appreciation for grace, and a willingness to tell the truth kindly and for the right reasons—which includes helping everyone involved become healthier, more effective leaders. Avoid advisors or friends who will tell you what they think you want to hear, and avoid foolish advisors who give full vent to whatever is stirring their spirit at the time. These "stirrings" are best described as opinions. In contrast, wise advisors quietly hold back their counsel for the appropriate time (Prov. 29:11). If all you want are opinions, head down to the closest bus stop—you'll find ten people standing there who will gladly share their opinion with you!

An effective outside advisor helps leaders understand and apply God's Word to the situation and to their relationships.

Philippians 2:1–4, for example, helps inform how we think about working with others:

> So if there is any encouragement in Christ,
> any comfort from love, any participation in the
> Spirit, any affection and sympathy, complete my
> joy by being of the same mind, having the same
> love, being in full accord and of one mind. Do
> nothing from selfish ambition or conceit, but
> in humility count others more significant than
> yourselves. Let each of you look not only to his
> own interests, but also to the interests of others.

In the heat of a difficult conflict these words might be tough to hear. But the right external advisor isn't concerned with saying things they hope will make you happy. In fact, they are okay if you "fire" them. They are not in a relationship with you for *your* glory, but rather for *God's* glory and for your *good*.

Think about how much conflict would end before it began if both parties stopped self-centered thinking and started looking for ways to humbly serve the other person. *What do* they *want? What do* they *need? What are* they *hoping for? What do* they *fear?*

It has been said that "true humility is not thinking less of yourself; it is thinking of yourself less."[26] The best advisors will point you toward Scripture and tell you the "kind truth." Seek these kinds of people as your closest friends and advisors—and don't "fire" them when they tell you hard things. If they are willing to tell you hard things, you can consider them a true friend (Prov. 27:6), and you can trust what they say.

---

26 Rick Warren, *The Purpose Driven Life* (Grand Rapids, MI: Zondervan, 2013, expanded edition).

Not all conflict needs an external advisor, but a healthy leader recognizes when help is needed and plans accordingly.

Right (and Wrong) Ways to Resolve Conflict

Returning to the earlier story of Matt and Rob, the good news is that they have grown in their respective roles and are now much more effective business partners and close friends.[27]

However, such growth was not automatic. There are some key ways *not* to resolve conflict. Lasting resolution requires a willingness to change the negative ways we handle conflict. One of the reasons organizational conflict can seem so pervasive and feel so stubborn is the fact that many leaders handle it the *wrong* way. The wrong way can be captured in an amusing—and fitting—acronym:

> **W**ithdraw from the conflict.
> **E**scalate the situation.
> **N**egatively interpret the situation.
> **I**nvalidate the other person.[28]

In other words, don't be a *weenie* about conflict.

Dealing with conflict ineffectively (WENI) is based in our human need to be in control. Withdrawing is perhaps the most natural response. When we are confronted with something unpleasant, it's an understandable reaction to want to walk away.

It's not surprising we sometimes handle conflict this way. After all, leaders are human.

---

27 For more on this, go to https://www.youtube.com/watch?v=4qYbWbDqzHA.

28 Scott M. Stanley, *A Lasting Promise* (San Francisco: Jossey-Bass, 2014).

What is important is that we not *continue* to handle conflict this way. We are loved by God, and it is our job to encourage others with our leadership.[29] When we remember this, the way we handle conflict is transformed. Instead of being a WENI, we engage, assume the best, and build others up. All of this is possible when we abide in Christ, and make His grace and truth part of our leadership.

Five Practical Steps Toward Resolving Conflict

Based on personal experiences internally at our organizations, as well as countless conversations we've had with leaders in other organizations, we'd like to provide five practical steps to consider on the journey toward resolving conflict.

Believe the best.

First, *believe the best*. As one of Matt's colleagues is fond of saying, "In the absence of information, people make it up."[30] Leaders crave information on which to base decisions. It is too easy, in the absence of information, to simply make something up to meet a perceived need. Unfortunately, our human nature may lead us to make up information that isn't helpful.

It may seem only natural to assign bad motives and bad intent, but that is not right or healthy for you or your relationships.

You have probably experienced conflict that takes place largely in your mind. Perhaps on the drive home from work, you recall a brief conversation or comment from one of your colleagues

---

29 Heb. 10:24–25.
30 Credit to David Dobat.

that struck you as "off," and you begin to attribute bad intent. When you pause to consider the *actual* conversation, however, rather than your assumptions, you can usually recognize such invented conflicts for what they are: harmful fictions.

Next time, instead of moving down the path of bad intent, move down the path of believing the best. If you force yourself to believe the best about your colleague, rather than negatively interpreting the situation, you will sleep better at night. Tomorrow, you can revisit the conversation and ask your colleague what they meant when they said "X." Nine times out of ten the conversation will be harmless and you won't have lost any sleep because you believed the best. If you take the opposite approach and assume bad things, your sleep and your relationships will suffer.

Confronting someone does not mean you must be *confrontational*

If you love your neighbor as yourself, you are doing right.[31] It is easy for us to believe the best about ourselves, and that is exactly how we ought to treat others, especially when we are in conflict.

Be direct and gracious.

Second, *be direct and gracious.* Confronting someone does not mean you must be *confrontational.*

Confront literally means to come "face to

---
31 James 2:8.

face" with someone. While it can have negative connotations, we are using the term to mean speaking directly with another person. *Confrontational*, on the other hand describes *how* someone addresses a problem: typically with hostility and/or aggression.

It is vital, then, that we consider our motives when we confront a problem. If our motive is anything but love, we need to ask *why* we want to confront the other person.

Unfortunately, leaders sometimes choose to confront conflict for selfish reasons, such as to prop up their own decisions or to attempt to manage their own reputation. However, conflict cannot be resolved unless the motivation of both parties is for the *other* person's best interest.

We've all heard of the Golden Rule, which comes from Matthew 7:12, part of Jesus' Sermon on the Mount: "So whatever you wish that others would do to you, do also to them."

There are times when we allow the so-called *silver* rule to guide us instead, which says, "Do *not* do to other people the things which you don't want done to you." But Jesus insisted on the Golden Rule. It is quite possible to imagine going for hours, days, or even weeks without doing something *actively* unpleasant or hateful to another person. Yet can we uphold the Golden Rule for even a single day? Can we do more than *avoid* harming the other person—can we work positively toward their health and nourishment?

Approach privately and in person.

Third, conflict resolution needs to happen *privately and in person*.

If your intent is to shame the other person in public or to protect your reputation, then go back and reread the first two points. One test of your motive is to ask whether you would feel satisfied to resolve the issue *entirely* in private. If part of you *wants* the issue to become public, then that should raise a red flag. Perhaps what you *really* want isn't a resolution, but to look better at the expense of the other person.

Similarly, it may be tempting to use email or a phone call for the conversation. However, despite the fact that such methods are private, *they fail to convey the full range of communication and emotion that healthy conflict resolution requires.* Sometimes we don't have the option of meeting in person, in which case we use technology as carefully and thoughtfully as we can. Too many times, however, an email or even a phone call has escalated an issue because of a misinterpretation.

As Matthew 18:15 says, "If your brother sins against you, go and tell him his fault, between you and him alone. If he listens to you, you have gained your brother." While this verse is written in the context of the *other* person's sin, it applies equally well to conflict. Resolution starts just between the two of you. So schedule the necessary time to sit down with the other person, face to face. That gives you the best chance to truly work things out, person to person.

Plan and prepare.

Fourth, conflict resolution requires *planning and preparation.*

In Wild West movies, often a gunslinger saunters through the swinging doors of a saloon, only to discover it is filled with enemies. Realizing it's an ambush, he jumps into action and guns start ablazing.

With conflict resolution, however, charging in and shooting from the hip is a recipe for disaster.

Instead, plan what you are going to say. *Practice* what you are going to say. It might sound ridiculous to rehearse a confrontation, but it's a good way to stay focused on the actual problem once you are in a meeting with the other person. Try to consider the responses your words will elicit, and what you might say in return. We've all been flustered in the midst of an intense conversation and lost the thread of our intended words—or worse, said rash words that deepened the conflict.

As you plan and prepare, be guided by your relationship with Jesus and the truth of His Word. "A soft answer turns away wrath, but a harsh word stirs up anger" (Prov. 15:1). And remember to let the truth of the previous points inform your thoughts. Believe the best. Be direct and gracious. Speak to the other person privately and in person. In other words, approach others the way *you* would want to be approached.

Forgive and rebuild.

Fifth, *forgive and rebuild trust.*

At any step in the process of conflict resolution, it can be extremely tempting to skip ahead
to when there is no longer a problem. However,
it is not possible to simply ignore the conflict and
move on, because true resolution comes *through*
the process, not in spite of the process.

Remember, you are ultimately responsible
for your own part in the conflict resolution.
While you *can* (and should) initiate the process
of conflict resolution, you cannot fix the other
person. You cannot force them to ask for forgiveness. You cannot coerce them into mending
a relationship.

Instead, you need to own *your* part, and
that requires *asking for forgiveness.*

There is a distinction between asking for
forgiveness and saying you are sorry. Despite
the way our culture uses the two words inter-
changeably, in reality they are different. Saying
you are sorry is insufficient, because all it recognizes is that you regret your behavior.

There are even times when saying "sorry"
can turn the responsibility back on the party
who was wronged. Have you ever said, "I'm
sorry *if* you felt that way"?

Such a statement casts doubt on your
willingness to take responsibility for *your* part
of the problem. Don't say "sorry" because you
think you are supposed to. Rather, seek reconciliation because you have seen the places where

you are at fault, and you want to correct them and work for unity and peace. By choosing the right words you can demonstrate you are genuinely interested in restoring trust in the relationship.

Forgiveness doesn't move past a conflict, but rather it *uses* the conflict as an opportunity to build a future relationship that is healthier and stronger. If someone were to communicate the following words, they would indicate a genuine desire to take responsibility and work toward reconciliation: *"I'm sorry for hurting you. Will you please forgive me? Is there anything I can do to make it up to you?"*

When you ask questions like this in an open-ended way, you are taking responsibility for your harmful actions *and* you are committing yourself to rebuild trust in the future. There is no wiggle room or uncertainty about whether you bear some of the blame. Additionally, you are giving up control and willingly allowing the other person to choose how they want to participate. You have invited them in and asked for their advice on how you can be a better friend to them next time. It is crucial to create a context in which you can make amends for the pain or difficulty you caused. Regaining trust and building friendship requires changed behaviors and attitudes in the future.

Conflict resolution is *not* about winning or getting what you want. Rather, *conflict resolution is about the greater good.* As

Hebrews 12:14 encourages, "Strive for peace with everyone, and for the holiness without which no one will see the Lord."

Approaching any conflict with the desire to come out ahead means missing the bigger opportunity. *Embracing* conflict, on the other hand, means coming to a place where you can move forward together. By doing so, you benefit your health, the other person's health, and the health of your organization.

The Pony Express

Scripture says that God allows tests and trials to come into our lives to teach us, to humble us, and to mature our faith. Proverbs 17:3 reminds us, "The crucible is for silver and the furnace is for gold, and the LORD tests the heart," while James 1:2–4 is even more direct:

> Count it all joy, my brothers, when you meet
> trials of various kinds, for you know that the
> testing of your faith produces steadfastness.
> And let steadfastness have its full effect, that
> you may be perfect and complete, lacking in
> nothing.

While we may wish these lessons could be learned in other ways, that is not typically how God works.

With that in mind, we'd like you to hear a story from Jeff about conflict. It occurred during a season in his life when God wanted to get his attention about an area of growth—and it had a profound effect on the way he now hires, manages, and develops people.

◆

I hadn't been in my position as missions director more than a few months when something curious happened: I found myself unable to fire a direct report. Having come from thirteen years in the legal world, I was unprepared for such a situation.

The new hire was supposed to fill a key role on my team. He was a high-capacity self-starter, initiator, and strategic thinker. However, after a few short weeks, it became clear that he was challenged by a "start up" mindset, often reflected by constantly shifting priorities. Looking back, I can see how unaware I was. Because I was continually redirecting him, he believed that he was unsuccessful. This led to some distrust and negative interpretation between us—classic WENI behavior.

After a few months, it became clear that we were not going to be able to continue to advance our organizational goals together unless something changed.

Normally, I would have simply called a meeting, laid out the facts (as *I* saw them), and released the employee. And I was planning to do so, until a senior leader at our church suggested a different course.

"Jeff," the leader told me, "we need to make sure our employee feels cared for, heard, and valued, whether he stays on your team or not." Talk about independent counsel—that was the last thing I wanted to hear!

As he explained it, I realized with a sinking feeling that it would be difficult, painful, and take much longer than I would like. In other words, I was about to move from the philosophical to the *practical execution* of biblical conflict resolution.

I wish I could say that I was excited about the prospect for personal growth. Nope. Not a bit, actually. It was a busy time at work, and I had a to-do list the length of my arm—not to mention a bold vision for what we wanted to accomplish as a team. My opinion of the proposed conflict resolution process was that it would not end well, and at the same time, it would distract all of us from what we were trying to accomplish.

That's when God put my heart to the test.

I knew the principles of biblical conflict resolution. I could even cite chapter and verse. The problem was that although I knew them, and had even taught them to others, I wasn't *living* them at work. When I began to actually work through the steps of conflict resolution, however, I grew more as a leader and a person than I could have imagined.

First I owned my part of the conflict, rather than blaming everything on my employee. Both of us were counseled by several objective friends. We slowly worked through steps like believing the best about each other, being direct and gracious, and keeping our conflict out of the public eye. I prepared and planned for conversations. And eventually, through a lengthy and at times difficult process, we forgave each other and began to build a relationship. It wasn't what I'd wanted to do, but by God's grace it turned out to be what I *needed* to do.

Looking back, I cringe at the thought of all I would have missed if I had taken the easy way out of a challenging situation. In that process I learned so much about myself, as well as vital lessons that shape the ways I craft job descriptions, hire, relate to my team, train, and lead.

I believe we need to lean into conflict. If we do the hard work of peeling back the onion, it transforms the way we view our organizations and our team members. God would have us lead in a way that testifies to the eternal value of every person. And if we lead in love, even through conflict, it transforms us in the process and makes us more like Him.

◆

When we make our tasks and goals preeminent, we forget that it is *people* who matter most and we set ourselves up for failure.

Whether in a church, a nonprofit, or a business, leaders may say that everything they are doing is about God's plan, God's purposes, and God's timing. Sometimes, however, those same leaders will realize they have stopped *walking with* Jesus and instead have started *working for* Jesus. The truth is that we work for God, not for other people, as Colossians 3:23–24 makes clear: "Whatever you do, work heartily, as for the Lord and not for men, knowing that from the Lord you will receive the inheritance as your reward." At the same time we are working as if God is our boss, we are walking with Jesus every day… and especially at work. It is only when we prioritize God that we can truly serve and lead people as God intends us to do.

Both of us have struggled with forgetting that serving people, not accomplishing tasks, needs to drive our work— which is why we love the following illustration.

When the Pony Express opened for business on April 3, 1860, it instantly transformed the way messages traveled across the continent.[32] If you had enough money, and you were in enough of a hurry, you could send a letter or a package from Missouri to California in a mere *ten* days, rather than several months.

The secret to such astounding speed? The brave riders and the ponies who carried them. More than 150 stations stretched

---

32 The Pony Express was made irrelevant by another forward-thinking idea—the telegraph—only eighteen months later.

across the continent, roughly one every ten miles, and the riders raced their mounts from point to point at nearly top speed, stopping only to exchange their tired pony for a rested and healthy one.

The riders were renowned for the bravery with which they guarded the pouches of mail which hung from their horse, and rightly so. If the mail was lost, customers would stop trusting the Pony Express with their business.

And yet the riders understood that adequately caring and providing for their ponies was just as important as protecting the mail. Sick, lame, or dead ponies meant no Pony Express—and no mail.

> No matter how important a given task or goal is, it cannot become more important than people.

No matter how important a given task or goal is, it cannot become more important than people. When you invest in your people, you'll have healthy relationships—and you'll *also* get stuff done. Invest in tasks at the expense of people, however, and all you'll have is a temporarily completed to-do list.

The Fight for Peace

As we close our discussion on why effective leaders resolve conflict, let's recall the bigger picture. Conflict resolution *is* difficult. However, as you develop this skill, both you *and* your organization will be healthier. And conflict resolution *must* begin with you.

Looking in the mirror can be painful, but as Romans 12:18 exhorts, "If possible, so far as it depends on you, live peaceably with all." As we saw in chapter 2, dealing with your *own* issues is more difficult than telling others what to do. There are long-term benefits to examining your own behavior.

By demonstrating to your team that you are ready and willing to consider your own role in the conflict, you build trust. Your team will see that you are committed to the facts and to the health of the organization, rather than to protecting your own interests. (Remember Philippians 2:3–4—"But in humility count others more significant than yourselves. Let each of you look not only to his own interests, but also to the interests of others.") Additionally, working on your own character and behavior will make future conflicts *less* likely and future friendships and partnerships *more* healthy and productive.

This will not happen without God's help. Second Corinthians 3:18 tells us that we "*are being transformed into the same image* from one degree of glory to another" (emphasis added). God never chooses to transform us into His image in the blink of an eye; it is a journey. When we put our trust in Jesus, we are saved instantly, but we become more like Jesus day by day, moment by moment, as we follow His commands and abide in His love.

As part of that process, consider making the following questions a periodic part of your self-assessment, even if you aren't in active conflict.

- Where have I created a lack of trust or confidence through my words or behavior?
- Where have I been wrong, or potentially wrong?
- Am I discussing things in an appropriate way?
- Am I abiding in Jesus, every day at work?

It isn't easy. And you have to swallow your pride. But in our experience, swallowing your pride is preferable to choking on it.

It is also helpful to regularly remind yourself that *conflict* is an opportunity, rather than something to be feared.

Recall from earlier how the conflict started between Matt and Rob: with a pride-fueled disagreement about who was "right" during a strategy session. Experiencing conflict is not bad, but allowing conflict to fester and poison relationships certainly is. What matters is that we deal with it in the best way possible.

The Bible tells us in Proverbs 27:17 that "iron sharpens iron, and one man sharpens another." Conflict can actually *unite* team members, as long as it forces them to come together to refine their work, develop their character, iterate their ideas, improve their attitudes, and so on.

Such a view of conflict is the result of a mature mindset. When leaders lean in to conflict, rather than pretending it doesn't exist, they open themselves up to many positive opportunities.

Both of us have experienced *significant* conflict at work, *and without that conflict our organizations would not be as healthy as they are today.* We've come to a place on our journey, in other words, where we are thankful for what conflict produces.

Resolving conflict in a healthy, biblical manner is invaluable to a thriving organization. You and your team will be better and more resilient when you proactively pursue peace.

Before that can happen, however, many of us need to overcome a significant roadblock: fear.

Discussion Questions:

1. List any "bricks" or "walls" of unresolved conflict that have been built in your organization.

2. Does your organization have a process in place to train others how to engage in effective conflict resolution?

3. Who would be a trustworthy external advisor you could invite into your life?

4. Have you ever handled conflict like a WENI? If so, what was the outcome?

5. Take some time to journal or pray through the five steps of effective conflict resolution.

"Why do you see the speck that is in your brother's eye, but do not notice the log that is in your own eye?"
(Matt. 7:3)

Chapter Four

FEAR

Overcoming the Wide Path

Jacob and Joseph are both important figures in the Old Testament, yet they led in very different ways.

One led selfishly, from behind, seeking to manipulate others into doing what he wanted. The other led selflessly, by example, seeking to honor God because he knew God would protect and provide. Both are vital characters in the story of God's people, and Genesis spends a great deal of time speaking about them.[33] Yet only one of them—Joseph—serves as a model for godly leaders.

That difference comes down to how they handled fear.

All leaders experience fear, but not all leaders are controlled by it. This is especially relevant as we make conflict resolution integral to the way we lead. Trusting God's sovereignty in all circumstances is difficult. Sometimes the pain of dealing with uncertainty causes us to question God and our circumstances. Sometimes we may not be convinced that trusting God and the role other people are playing will truly benefit us.

Fear is understandable, but we cannot allow it to determine our leadership.

---

33 You can read the story of Jacob in Genesis 25–36, and the story of Joseph in Genesis 37–50.

Fear limits our development, both personally and professionally. When we cease to trust God fully, fear begins to permeate our lives. Fear can produce more fear, and soon we can find ourselves unable (or unwilling) to trust that what God says is true. Those who are controlled by fear avoid dealing with the facts. Instead, they want to deal with a version of the truth that allows them to stay in a place of comfort, pleasure, or power.

Fear can be a significant roadblock because it can show up in so many places. Many of us have fear "blind spots" that can keep us at the crossroads, unwilling to move forward.

However, leaders who are willing to deal with the reality of their situation can confront fear because they know God controls the outcome. That is the fruit of trust: we can have peace even in the midst of fear, knowing our abiding relationship with Christ will always result in our growth and impact.

Fear of Failure

Many people fear failure. That fear can make leaders hesitant to attempt something unless they know they will succeed.

However, effective leaders know failure will happen at times. Both personal failure and failure from their employees. Why? Because people who never fail are people who aren't growing by pushing themselves into uncomfortable situations.

This is true in every area of life. The athlete who never fails will not improve. The artist who never fails will produce only uninspiring art. Expecting someone to avoid failure means expecting that person to never grow.

Fearing failure isn't surprising. Many of us were raised to hide our failure, and we've carried that mindset into adulthood. High achievers are taught "failure is not an option." Yet this narrative needs to change if we want a generation of leaders willing to fail. Think of people God used significantly in the Bible, such as Peter, David, Paul, Abraham, Gideon, Mary, Paul, Isaiah, Elijah. All overcame significant fear or failure.

Remember, God doesn't expect us to succeed every time, but rather to be dependent on Him and trust Him. If you are pushing yourself to the limit, keeping a great attitude, and honoring God with your choices, it is okay if failure is part of the process God uses to mold you into the man or woman He desires you to be. God delights in redeeming what seems unredeemable.

Fear of failure will limit our development spiritually. It is ironic that we attempt to hide our failure from God. God is the only one who knows our failures better than we do, yet who loves us unconditionally.

> **Failure often provides our greatest moments of learning and development.**

Failure often provides our greatest moments of learning and development. Matt likes to ask his kids, "How did you fail today?" If they failed, he and his wife encourage them to continue to take appropriate risks. If they didn't fail, he asks what they can do tomorrow to step out and try something new or challenging. It could be as simple as failing on the final rep of a difficult workout, or failing to get a role in the school play. The point is to train the kids to appreciate failure as both an indicator of courage and as a teacher, which is the same lesson we need to model for our organizations.

Jacob feared failure. He was terrified that he would not succeed in life without the birthright and blessing that belonged to his brother. In his fear, he lied to his father and manipulated his brother, hoping to protect himself and "guarantee" his success.

Joseph presents a counter-example. Try to imagine yourself in his place. You are in jail for a crime you didn't commit.

Your career is finished. Your credibility and reputation are shot. Then one day, out of nowhere, the CEO of America's largest corporation pays your bail and asks to meet with you personally. He believes you might be able to help him solve his business problem. You do, in fact, understand his problem. But the solution will be extremely painful. No one has dared to share it with him. Provisionally free from jail, the very last thing you want to do is give him bad news about his business.

This is exactly what Joseph does. Despite his fear, Joseph delivers the hard news. Pharaoh has the power to make or break Joseph, but Joseph trusts God. He knows Pharaoh is not responsible for his life, and God is ultimately in control.

Faithful leaders speak the truth, especially when it isn't in their own self-interest.

Fear of Others

Fearing what others think about us will undermine our leadership.

Whenever we put more value in what others say or think about us than in what God says or *knows* about us, we allow fear to minimize our influence.

In John 12:42–43 we read about several leaders who could have changed their community, but instead they became distracted. They seek the approval of people who were viewed as influential, rather than the approval of God.

> Whenever we put more value in what others say or think about us than in what God says or *knows* about us, we allow fear to minimize our influence.

"Nevertheless many even of the authorities believed in [Jesus], but for fear of the Pharisees they did not confess it, so that they would not be put out of the synagogue; for they loved the glory that comes from man more than the glory that comes from God."

These leaders had listened to Jesus teach, and believed He was the Messiah. Yet fear kept them from choosing God's way. Imagine the difference they could have made if they'd trusted the words of Jesus enough to confess Him publicly.

In our culture, we too are tempted to choose the approval of men rather than the approval of God. Have you ever:

- Refrained from mentioning your faith in a business conversation?
- Spent emotional energy wondering what other people think about you?
- Spoken with the intent of making yourself look good?
- Cared more about what "important" people thought of you than "unimportant" ones?

Fearing others, as we read in Proverbs 29:25, "lays a snare, but whoever trusts in the LORD is safe."

Jacob's deceitful actions caused a serious rift in his family, to the point where his brother wanted to kill him. Decades later, Jacob's fear of his brother remained so strong that he sent his family and flocks ahead of him, hoping they would act as a buffer to his brother's anger. Rather than solve his conflict with his brother, and deal with the reality of his situation, Jacob chose to hide behind his fear.

Joseph, on the other hand, did not seek the "glory that comes from man." While serving in a high position for a powerful man, Joseph was falsely accused of adultery. Despite being thrown into prison, Joseph trusted God. He did not allow his fear to compromise his leadership and integrity, and he did not seek to bargain his way out of an unjust punishment. In time his faithfulness was rewarded, and the scope of his leadership increased exponentially.

Emotional and Spiritual Fear

Fear presents itself in many forms, all of which are crippling. We may defeat fear in one area of our lives, only to have it appear somewhere else.

- The fear of losing someone can prevent us from making a godly decision.
- The fear of pain can make us hesitant to take a necessary risk.
- The fear of discomfort can tempt us to take shortcuts.
- The fear of being fully known can hamper our relationships with others and with God as we try to present a "cleaned up" version of ourselves.
- The fear of loneliness can tempt us into harmful relationships.

This list could go on and on. Regardless of the particular fear, refusing to trust God is our way of saying we know better.

We think our way makes more sense. We may not admit to believing this, but the truth of our beliefs is demonstrated by our behavior. Anytime we choose to act in a way that is inconsistent with God's way, we allow fear to say we know better than God.

The Antidote to Fear

Fear is a threat to healthy leadership, but we are never helpless. Fear need not paralyze us. The antidote to fear is to trust God's promises, even if we cannot see how they will be accomplished.

When we trust that what God says is true, and that what God says will happen, we no longer have a reason to let fear control our lives. Romans 8:31–32 says, "If God is for us, who can be against us? He who did not spare his own Son but gave him up for us all, how will he not also with him graciously give us all things?" God promises that all the resources we need to overcome a particular situation will be made available to us.

And with trust comes abiding love. If fear is the reason we fail to act, love is the reason we choose to act. First John 4:18 says, "There is no fear in love, but perfect love casts out fear. For fear has to do with punishment, and whoever fears has not been perfected in love." God's love is made perfect in us, through Christ.

Returning to our biblical example, it seems as if Jacob's entire life was controlled by fear. Through the providence and grace of God, Jacob was still able to be part of great endeavors, yet imagine his potential impact if he had trusted instead of feared. Trusting is exactly what Joseph did. His steadfast trust in God may have seemed unreasonable when his brothers left him for dead, or when he was forgotten in Pharaoh's dungeons, but God used him mightily and in unimaginable ways.

With that in mind, consider the differences between leaders who are takers and those who are givers. Givers like Joseph are rare and valuable, while takers like Jacob are plentiful and difficult. Takers are controlled by fear and manipulate others, while givers trust God in all circumstances.

We see some of these differences in the lives of Jacob and Joseph, and all of us have experienced these differences in our organizations.

The qualities of a taker:

- Tends to tell half-truths (e.g., résumés, rumors, circumstances, etc.) and avoids unbecoming facts
- Shows favoritism to those who can help the most
- Willing to compromise their integrity to achieve a desired outcome
- Tends to damage or frustrate close relationships
- Either passive or overly aggressive behavior when working through an issue
- Criticizes others, takes credit
- Unwilling to change and resists new ideas
- Behaves inconsistently (i.e., best friend one day, nemesis the next)
- Gossips, with no intent of going directly to person in question
- Resists difficult assignments, waits to be asked, does less than required
- Sense of entitlement and lack of gratitude

A giver, on the other hand:

- Tells the truth, is fact based, and works hard to be objective and unbiased
- Treats people fairly regardless of position, title, or influence
- Handles difficult situations, issues, or conflict directly
- Initiates candid conversations with the intent of helping everyone grow
- Does not tolerate gossip or discussing others behind their back

- Passes on the credit and praises and encourages others, both publicly and privately
- Flexible and willing to change behavior when helpful
- Enjoys learning new things
- Willing to do jobs "beneath" them
- Consistent in both words and behaviors
- Has admirable character qualities that build trust and loyalty
- Looks for ways to serve others
- Sense of gratitude and a thankful demeanor and spirit

We've all been givers and takers at times. It is never fun to work with a taker, and even when takers are productive, their gains tend to be selfish and shortsighted.

One of the most powerful things we can do for our colleagues, friends, and family is to grow in our generosity and resist the temptation to slip into the mindset of a taker. Fear drives us to care for ourselves above all else. Love has an "others first" mindset, and the behaviors that follow are counterintuitive but helpful.

Your health and effectiveness as a leader is directly connected to your willingness to deal with facts. The facts

> God is at work in and through you, so fear need not rule you.

of your organization are critical, such as the personal, professional, relational, emotional, and financial realities you must confront. You cannot make good decisions unless they are based in facts. Fear wants to pull you away from doing that.

The facts should drive us to Jesus and abiding in Christ. Jesus must be the foundation. Not only will you learn to work through conflict, but you will move past your fear and become a giver. Your relationships in your organization will be characterized by unity, generosity, and discipleship.

God is at work in and through you, so fear need not rule you. Ecclesiastes 11 teaches that some of what we do as leaders is *meant* to fail. God does not ask us to be perfect, but to be faithful as we walk toward Him. There is no fear in faithfulness. And as we explore in the next chapter, *healthy relationships bear significant fruit.*

Discussion Questions:

1. How have you allowed fear to influence your thoughts and actions? What was the outcome?

2. How can fear of failure limit your spiritual growth? What is the antidote?

3. The business world can pressure us to seek the approval of people, rather than the approval of God. When has this happened to you?

4. Is your organization staffed with more "givers" or "takers"? How are you doing in this area?

5. Spend some time in God's Word, looking at His promises. Which ones do you need to claim and trust?

"There is no fear in love. But perfect love casts out fear. For fear has to do with punishment, and whoever fears has not been perfected in love." (1 John 4:18)

Chapter Five

RELATIONSHIPS

Journeying Together

Workplace friendships are vital.

Some of the world's best-known and most respected organizations prioritize relationships. Facebook's Mark Zuckerberg, for example, places a high business value on relationships. "We have a tradition," he writes, "where every Friday we have a Q&A and all employees can come and ask me questions about anything they want." Zuckerberg also does this with customers and journalists via "Q&A with Mark" sessions.[34]

Relationships do not happen by accident. You must build touch points with key relationships into your schedule. The benefits of great relationships are subjective but significant:

Leaders ...
- Trust their teams and reduce micromanaging
- Improve retention and lengthen their best working relationships
- Enjoy developing friendships while engaging in challenging work

---

34 Mark Zuckerberg, Facebook Post, October 30, 2014, https://www.facebook.com/zuck/posts/10101719793886061

Team members ...
- Trust each other rather than compete with each other
- Work harder because they care more
- Enjoy seeing their coworkers succeed

Clients ...
- Work with friends instead of "vendors"
- Develop trust with third-party providers
- Enjoy their work and are loyal to proven third-party providers

Prioritizing relationships isn't just good for you as a leader, but also as a person. This is captured in a hand-illustrated sign Matt keeps near his desk: *Love what you do, love who you do it with, love who you come home to.*

Love what you do.

This is your craft and calling, not merely your "job." There is something you are better at than most people, and you enjoy pouring energy, time, and thought into it. When you execute your craft well, it makes a significant positive contribution. Work is enjoyable when we know it is making a difference and an impact. And excellence both inspires people and honors God.

Love what you do, love who you do it with, love who you come home to.

For example, Matt loves marketing, in part because he believes it is the amplifier of the reality of what is really going on in an organization. He loves to use marketing to help others discover and appreciate great work that has been accomplished, the great people who did it, and how it has ultimately helped their friends. When others hear the amplified sound of great work, they want more of it. So his firm grows, and as it builds into more leaders and is able to be more generous, as Matt likes to say, "our little corner of the world begins to change."

This is the sort of tangible benefit that flows naturally from loving what you do.

Love who you do it with.

This has a double meaning that is incredibly important. As we've shared in previous chapters, we love the people we get to work with—and sometimes we even tell them that at work! That may sound strange, but everyone needs to know they are loved. We work with incredibly smart, diligent, hard-working, and honorable people who have something unique and great to offer. We enjoy working with folks like that, and we want to acknowledge them.

The double meaning of loving who you work with is the act of caring for them. We greatly enjoy opportunities to help our friends at work, using whatever resources we have to meet a legitimate need. For example, a friend of Jeff's was asked to preach a wedding—something he had never done before. The church's marriage team coached him and practiced with him, and

a few others from the team took him out to buy
him a suit. He'd never owned one before and
was excited to discover that the pants came *with*
the jacket! Everyone involved in helping him was
delighted to be part of the process of caring.

Love who you come home to.

This has the same crucial double meaning: you can
love and enjoy coming home to your family, whatever size/shape it is, *and* make sure you are actively
loving your family.

Even if you are single, it is a mistake to
be "unattached." Just as we are meant to abide
in Christ through every season of life, we are
meant to actively love friends, neighbors, and
even strangers.

The best part of this is the reinforcement
between who you are at work and who you are
at home. You are meant to be the same person,
all the time. If you feel that you need to be *one*
person at work, and *another* person at home,
take that as a warning sign that your relationships are not yet biblically healthy.

In other words, *love what you do, love who
you do it with, and love who you come home to.*

Work relationships can and should be fun. Not simply
when "goofing off," but also while accomplishing real work
with team members and clients. Learn how to develop meaningful workplace relationships *now*, instead of waiting until
"you have more time" or "things settle down." The near and
long-term benefits are immeasurable.

Some assume that friendships don't belong in the workplace. At best friendships are a distraction. At worst they hinder the organization's goals. In contrast, we believe that healthy workplace friendships make leaders stronger and more effective, team members happier and more fulfilled, and a company culture that is sustainable and generous. After all, we typically spend more time per week with our colleagues than with our families.

If you want to have an incredibly rewarding life, at work *and* at home, help your friends and have lots of them.

The Importance of Workplace Friendships

Matt's company recently held their semiannual "State of the Office" meeting. In addition to discussing the normal agenda, such as financial strategy, promotions, client stories, and so on, Matt's business partner Rob stated, "The partners here don't just strive to achieve *unity* as a team...we also work diligently on our *friendships*."

That comment surprised some of the newer team members. How could the leaders have time to work on friendship? Why was that so

Friendships infuse work with meaning.

important? Weren't there more impactful things they could spend their time on? We'll let the words of one of those newer team members answer the question.

> My colleagues at work have become great friends. They inspire me, push me toward excellence, encourage me, and support me. When I am struggling, they step up to help me without any expectations. And when things are going

great, they are the first to celebrate with me.
They are a huge part of the reason why I love to
come to work every day.[35]

We couldn't say it better. Here are two ways that relationships make someone "love to come to work every day."

First, friendships infuse work with meaning. Writing for *Harvard Business Review*, Tamara Erickson points out that employees are often "less motivated by money than by the connection they feel at work."[36] And not only do workplace friendships provide motivation, job satisfaction, and increased productivity, but they increase retention. "While companies often pay significant attention to the loyalty employees feel toward the organization, the best employers recognize that loyalty also exists among employees toward one another."[37] Surprisingly, the same study reveals that one of the primary characteristics of a great workplace is one where employees respond affirmatively to this statement: "I have a best friend at work."

Returning to Erickson's findings, "[meaning is] what people are looking for at work. Clear company values, translated into the day-to-day work experience, are one of the strongest drivers of an engaged workforce, one primed for successful collaboration." And employees who work "in a world of extended collaboration" are more "excited and enthusiastic

---

35 Morgan Eseke, http://www.credera.com/blog/
management-consulting/relationships-series-introduction/.
36 Tammy Erickson, "Meaning Is the New Money," *Harvard Business Review*, March 23, 2011, https://hbr.org/2011/03/challenging-our-deeply-held-as/.
37 "Based on Gallup Research: What Makes a Great Workplace?" http://thepeoplegroup.com/wp-content/uploads/2008/04/article-gallup-research-what-makes-a-great-workplace1.pdf.

about that they're doing... [T]hey invite others in and are emotionally contagious. Engaged employees identify proudly with the organization and their work."

What would your organization be like if your team began to collaborate and relate more often? What can you do to create an environment that increases that likelihood? You can certainly encourage it, *but engagement will not last unless it grows organically out of a genuine desire for workplace relationships.*

That starts with you. The soil for growth can be prepared by the leader who is abiding with Christ, living out biblical principles and in investing deeply in workplace friendships. If *you* are not doing it, why would anyone else?

Second, friendships at work do more than make the overall culture better. Friendships make *you* better. If you have a close friend at work, both your performance and your character will be better than if you were alone. Friends rejoice in each other's success, even as they are spurred to work harder on themselves. Just as long-distance runners travel farther together and celebrate the end of a long run together, colleagues who are friends encourage each other toward greatness.

Friends at work do more than challenge us to be better at a particular job or skill. They *correct* us. A company culture that encourages workplace friendships is not a serene environment with daily chants of "Kumbaya." As Proverbs 27:6 says, "Faithful are the wounds of a friend; profuse are the kisses of an enemy." Friends share the truth with each other, even when it hurts.

It is possible and worthwhile to develop a family-like culture in your organization. Your entire team can become better and more effective. The idea of "helping your friends" can influence your interactions with team members and clients, and ultimately lead to a healthier organization.

Viewing Customers as Friends

Admirable businesses don't chase sales or dollars. Rather, they find valuable ways to help their friends (i.e., customers!).

In his insightful book *Every Good Endeavor: Connecting Your Work to God's Work*, Tim Keller writes that such a business would be characterized by:

- A discernible vision for serving the customer in some unique way
- A lack of adversarial relationships and exploitation
- An extremely strong emphasis on excellence and product quality
- An ethical environment that goes 'all the way down' to the bottom of the organizational chart and to the realities of daily behavior, even when high ethics mean a loss of margin[38]

Do you think such a business would normally be profitable? We do. Profit is very important because it clearly indicates the customer's interest in allowing the business to continue to provide goods or services to the marketplace in its current form. It affirms the value of the goods or services we provide and is a key way we "love our neighbors" in our community. Without profit, the business will eventually die.

That is why business development must be based on helping people. It cannot be based on manipulating someone into buying something. Scott Covington, one of the partners at Matt's company, has eight to ten "business development" meetings per week, and he puts it like this: "It all boils down

---

38 Tim Keller, *Every Good Endeavor: Connecting Your Work to God's Work* (New York: Penguin Books, 2014).

to people and I find great joy in building great relationships and helping my friends."

A genuine desire to help others leads to long-lasting partnerships. Partnerships are based on trust and an agreement to achieve a common goal. Healthy relationships between people take priority over contracts between corporations. If someone pulls out the contract to see what it says, chances are a promise is not being kept and the relationship isn't working. Contracts are intended to provide clarity on the intentions of the relationship, and no one consults the contract if the person they are working with is fulfilling their promises.

With that in mind, here are four principles for friendship that *also* apply to serving customers.

- *A friendship is others-focused.* Friends prioritize the needs of others and genuinely desire what is best for the people they care about. What would happen if your organization treated customers that way? Rather than focusing on what others can provide you, focus on what others need and on how you can help them achieve that.
  For example, Matt's company is "technology agnostic." Not owing allegiance to a particular software or hardware system means they can provide unbiased recommendations.
- *Friends are honest with each other.* Lip service or half-truths have no place in friendship. If you are advising a customer, sometimes you will have to share difficult facts. Managing information, limiting, or censoring your feedback

in order to win or keep a contract is not something a true friend would do.

For example, are you willing to advise a
potential customer that *your* organization is not
the best fit for their needs?

- *Friends share common goals and interests.* Helping
a customer achieve a goal you do not believe in
is a form of manipulation. We know a company
that turned down a million-dollar contract
because they didn't believe the mechanics of the
customer's business model were ethical. On the
other hand, if you understand and share a customer's dreams, you can work together toward a
common goal.

- *Friends have fun together.* Do you make it a goal
to actually *enjoy* spending time with the people
you are doing business with? Weaving fun into
your experiences with your customers means
that you will get more done and enjoy doing it.
Fun and laughter are an integral part of genuine workplace relationships.

For example, a client chose an unusual way
to thank one of Matt's team members for his
excellent work on a long-term project—sending
a singing gorilla to serenade him at the office in
front of all of his friends!

It is critical to note that building friendships *cannot be
faked.* Viewing these ideas as "sales techniques" destroys the
entire point. If your motive is self-serving, you are merely
manipulating.

The Team That Laughs Together...

In the not too distant past, a tall, lanky man dressed in a wetsuit, flippers, and goggles made his way across the gaming floor of a casino in the Bahamas. The startled patrons looked up from their drinks or the game they were playing and wondered what was going on. The mystery deepened when the man stopped in front of a woman who was smoking. Asking the woman to give him her cigarette, he proclaimed, "I'm Captain Snorkel, and I'm fighting cancer one cigarette at a time—would you like to donate to the cause?"

He repeated this line each time he flopped toward a smoking guest. Clearly he was either mentally unstable, or had lost a bet.

It turns out it was the latter, and that Captain Snorkel was none other than Matt, having a ton of fun with his team members—and building relationships and memories along the way.

As Dwight D. Eisenhower noted, "A sense of humor is part of the art of leadership, of getting along with people, of getting things done." Humor is often overlooked, but having fun together is essential to cultivating a great company culture. (And for what it's worth, it doesn't have to start with something as extreme as Captain Snorkel!)

Playing games together, common areas stocked with drinks and snacks that draw employees together, a regular after-work happy hour, white-elephant gift exchanges—the fun ways to get together and encourage friendship and laughter are nearly infinite.

A word of caution: fun can't be forced. The desire to enjoy spending time together must be shared and organic.

And this isn't something to "tack on" to your organization merely so people have more fun. As Mike Kerr notes in *The Humor Advantage: Why Some Businesses Are Laughing All the Way to the Bank*, "humor is a key ingredient in creative thinking. It helps people play with ideas, lower their internal critic, and see things in new ways."[39]

Sometimes fun events expand into company-wide events, like trips to the ballpark, service days (which we'll talk more about in chapter 6), and even destination trips. For example, every year the financial goals are met at Matt's company, the team members take an all-expenses-paid trip, spouses included, to a fun destination like the Bahamas, New Orleans, or San Francisco. Beyond the motivational element, trips represent an investment in the culture and future of an organization. Team members return from these trips with lasting memories, deeper friendships, and an excitement to make the following year better.

Listen to the way one of Matt's employees describes it:

> Having fun together strengthens our work
> relationships and breaks down barriers to
> communication. When our leadership team
> shows they are able to cut loose and have fun
> (even if they look like total idiots while doing
> it), I actually respect them more. Fun and
> laughter tend to flatten the hierarchy and foster
> communication and innovation. As a junior
> level employee, I have ample opportunities to
> engage with our partner team in a fun, relaxed

---

39 "3 Reasons Why Humor Should Be Part of Your Leadership Toolkit," Center for Executive Excellence, September 5, 2013, http://executiveexcellence.com/funny-business-3-reasons-humor-part-leadership-toolkit.

level at monthly happy hours or at company events. I have been able to build friendships not only with my peers but also with our leadership team, and it's easy to share ideas and helpful feedback with your friends.[40]

Or consider the way Jeff's church has transformed the simple dice game of Farkle into an organization-wide relationship builder.

We have a lot of hilariously fun traditions at our church, from staff play days where we have kick-ball and laser tag competitions to prizes awarded at staff meetings to anyone who can say everyone's name—and we have over 180 people! My favorite, however, are the crazy set of memories connected to the game of Farkle. Our team will use nearly any excuse to play the ordinary game, but the outcomes are always extraordinary. For example, Farkle losers have had to do things that include:

- Holding up a live chicken every hour on the hour during a staff retreat, and reciting a fact about chickens.
- Swim once a week in the outside baptismal pond at church, regardless of the weather.
- Face an "ice bucket" challenge in which all the water is replaced by the food scraps and liquid waste from 100 people eating lunch.

40 Morgan Eseke, "It's All About Relationships Part 4: Laughing Together," February 3, 2014, https://www.credera.com/blog/management-consulting/relationships-part-4-laughing-together/.

- Stand in the lobby of church dressed as a mascot from a sports team they hate.

As you can see, a simple game can provide some pretty epic bonding! And I can't resist telling one more story about a recent staff Christmas party. My wife and son lost their respective games, and the punishment was hysterical—at least to me. First they had to take a swim outside in a near-freezing pond. Then they were rolled in flour and their teams had to decorate them as gingerbread cookies, complete with syrup, pieces of candy, and frosting.

Our pastor comes from a background in Christian camps, like Kanakuk, so a large part of our culture is staff bonding, deep relationships, and fun together. When I first came into this environment from the business world, I remember thinking how hokey some of it seemed. Now I can't imagine a team culture that isn't about fun relationships. After all, you spend more time with your coworkers than your own family, so you might as well enjoy each other.

A team that laughs together tends to build great relationships. Teams who genuinely like each other accomplish more together.

Why Some Leaders Fail to Invest in Relationships

We have shared solid third-party *data* confirming the value of healthy workplace relationships, but we understand this from personal *experience* as well. Many of us have had a friendship that is both life-changing and life-giving. Proverbs speaks to conversations that change the lives of those we love:

- There is one whose rash words are like sword thrusts, but the tongue of the wise brings heal-ing. (Prov. 12:18)
- Whoever goes about slandering reveals secrets; therefore do not associate with a simple babbler. (Prov. 20:19)
- Oil and perfume make the heart glad, and the sweetness of a friend comes from his earnest counsel. (Prov. 27:9)

The writers of the New Testament discuss relationships often. They understood that any healthy organization or community, such as the burgeoning church, needed to focus on the right way to treat each other. Going it alone wasn't an option. Consider these verses:

- Let love be genuine. Abhor what is evil; hold fast to what is good. Love one another with brotherly affection. Outdo one another in showing honor. (Rom. 12:9–10)
- Never pay back evil for evil to anyone. Do things in such a way that everyone can see you are honorable. (Rom. 12:17)
- Be kind to one other, tenderhearted, forgiving one another, as God in Christ forgave you. (Eph. 4:32)
- Therefore encourage one another and build one another up. (1 Thess. 5:11)

- Above all, keep loving one another earnestly,
  since love covers a multitude of sins. (1 Pet. 4:8)
- My beloved brothers: let every person be quick to
  hear, slow to speak, slow to anger. (James 1:19)

And this is only a small sampling of God's teaching
about relationships. Jesus spoke often about the subject, and
when asked to summarize all of the Old Testament law, He
responded by saying, "'Love the Lord your God with all your
heart and with all your soul and with all your mind. This is
the great and first commandment. And a second is like it: You
shall love your neighbor as yourself. On these two command-
ments depend all the Law and the Prophets" (Matt. 22:37–40).

In other words, if you are a leader who is also following
Christ, you *must* pursue workplace relationships. Why then,
if such friendships are incredibly beneficial *and* biblical, don't
more leaders invest in and prioritize them?

Because the truth about relationships can be obscured
by lies.

Some lies about relationships are little more than out-
dated business axioms, while other lies are more destructive
because they have a spiritual dimension. Ephesians 6:11–12
instructs believers to "Put on the whole armor of God, that
you may be able to stand against the schemes of the devil.
For we do not wrestle against flesh and blood, but against
the rulers, against the authorities, against the cosmic pow-
ers over this present darkness, against the spiritual forces
of evil in the heavenly places." It is often viewed as naive
or uninformed in our secular culture to connect our daily
activities to an unseen realm of spiritual power and to what
happens in our hearts. Nevertheless, there is a link between
what God says, what we believe, and how we act.

Consider the following common lies.

- *"Hard-charging leaders are better for the company."* This lie has probably been around as long as there have been companies. The mistaken belief is that a leader needs to drive forward, not stopping for anything or any*one*, for the company to succeed. The reality, however, is that healthy *people* are far more predictive of a company's success. No matter how capable and hardworking a single leader is, a single leader can only do so much without unified buy-in from team members.

- *"My ideas are usually the best ones."* This lie is typically unspoken. It is more of a subtle temptation than a direct belief. Every idea I have in isolation *seems* like a great one, but that doesn't make it true. Leaders don't normally arrive at their positions of influence by accident, but rather through hard work and merit. So there is *some* truth to the idea that their ideas may be good ones. Confronted with a choice between a quick individual decision and the longer process of seeking input via a network of relationships, many leaders choose the easy route.

- *"This organization matters more than any individual in it."* This lie masquerades as a truth by sounding humble. Since it implies that we're keeping the focus on something *bigger* than ourselves, it seems to be correct. It is especially believable when the organization is accomplishing good things in the world. At the heart of that statement, however, is the lie that a business can be more important than a person. *The truth is that no business is eternal, but every person is.*

We seldom think in these terms. Yet as Rick Warren writes,

You're not going to take your career with you to Heaven, but you are going to take your character. And while you are here on Earth, God is developing your character and testing your faithfulness. Will you be faithful to do the right thing, even when you don't feel like doing the right thing? He's watching so that he can determine what kind of job he is going to give you in eternity. Jesus said in Luke 16:10-12, "Whoever can be trusted with very little can also be trusted with much… So if you have not been trustworthy in handling worldly wealth, who will trust you with true riches? And if you have not been trustworthy with someone else's property, who will give you property of your own?"[41]

Warren's focus is on the individual here, but we must also remember that God is using leaders like you to develop *other* people's character and faithfulness as well. As we will see in chapter 6, the ultimate "business" of your organization is discipleship.

- *"The pain, difficulty, and frustration of community just isn't worth it."* In the Christian life, isolation is always a danger. We may have heard

---

41 Rick Warren, "God Uses Your Work to Develop Your Character," *Pastor Rick's Daily Hope*, April 7, 2015, http://rickwarren.org/devotional/english/god-uses-your-work-to-develop-your-character.

> stories of ultra-holy monastic types who lived
> in a cave alone for decades, prayed seven hours
> a day, and memorized the entire Bible. It is
> not our place to discuss or even evaluate such
> forms of spirituality here. If you are reading
> this, however, we are confident that you are not
> living in a cave! In the Christian life, you miss
> out on opportunities for growth, joy, compan-
> ionship, and faithfulness when you are isolated.

Abiding in Christ is the only sustainable way to combat such lies and get back on a healthy track. Never forget who you really are and where you are going. Just as a passport enables you to travel to many different places, it also clearly communicates the country that is your home and your citizenship. Regardless of your past or present, you are an eternal child of God. If you choose to love and follow Jesus, your destiny is eternal joy, alongside all of God's children. Those truths provide perspective to whatever you are dealing with as a leader, just as they encourage you to prioritize relationships.

Lessons of Relational Leadership

Your organization exists as a *relay* race, not an individual race.

Your job is to hand the baton to others, via relationships, and then to cheer them on. Pass on the values and the truth that God has trusted you with. Someone *will* run the last leg at your organization, but it will likely not be you.

Read 2 Timothy 2:2 as if you are speaking it to your team: "What you have heard from me in the presence of many witnesses entrust to faithful men, who will be able to teach others also."

We understand this truth at a gut level when it comes to our families. We pass on values and truth from generation to generation. But it is equally true at work. Remember, people are the *only* eternal investment on earth. The friendships you create and cultivate matter in this life and in eternity.

Work *is* transformative. How is your work transforming you, and vice versa? Does your work make you more likely to gossip? How focused are you on getting what you think you deserve at work? Does your work make you more or less likely to be peaceful, humble, coachable, and generous?

If you treat your team as you would like to be treated, friendships take root *and* you will have a ton of fun along the way.

> When you invest in friendships with employees, clients, and industry partners, you give your organization its best chance to succeed.

So many times, we as leaders give speeches and talks about the principles that support our work. But relationships are where we must live those principles out. It is in our relationships that others will learn whether we are about talk or about action.

Relationships are the currency of our culture. When you invest in friendships with employees, clients, and industry partners, you give your organization its best chance to succeed. And regardless of the level of success, you will be investing in something that will last forever.

So on your journey, help your friends, and have lots of them. It isn't just the right thing for your business. It's what Christ is calling you to do.

Which benefit of healthy workplace relationships do you think would be most useful in your organization?

Discussion Questions:

1. Have you cultivated great workplace relationships? If not, what has held you back?

2. Are there ways you could help your friends at work more?

3. Consider the four principles of friendship. Is there one that you need to focus on?

4. Which lies about workplace friendships have you believed?

"This is my commandment, that you love one another as I have loved you. Greater love has no one than this, that someone lay down his life for his friends. You are my friends if you do what I command you. No longer do I call you servants, for the servant does not know what his master is doing; but I have called you friends, for all that I have heard from my Father I have made known to you." (John 15:12–15)

Chapter Six

UNITY

Better Together

William Wilberforce (1759–1833) is one of our heroes. A member of the British Parliament, he is best known for the abolition of the Atlantic slave trade in Britain. Beginning in the mid-fifteenth century, and peaking at the end of the eighteenth century, more than eleven million Africans were taken from their native countries and forced into slavery in the Americas. During the eighteenth century alone, six million Africans were captured and taken to the Americas—and Britain was responsible for more than 40 percent of those slaves.

Wilberforce began his work in 1787, *but the Atlantic slave trade wasn't officially abolished until 1807.*[42]

How could one man work for so long on such an overwhelmingly complicated and seemingly intractable problem?

He couldn't. Wilberforce didn't do it alone. He surrounded himself with friends, family members, colleagues, sympathetic political figures, writers, business leaders, and artists—in short, with the team he needed to get the job done.

---

42 The United States voted to abolish the Atlantic slave trade that same year, yet its internal slave trade remained legal in most southern states until the 1860s.

Consider the work Wilberforce and his team undertook, year after year. Drafting and supporting legislation. Hosting debates. Preaching sermons. Passing out pamphlets. Wrangling for votes. Preparing for and giving speeches. Writing letters. Attending prayer meetings. Raising funds. Studying Scripture. This was the seemingly unending work of countless people that took *two decades* to bear fruit.

Now known as the Clapham Sect, Wilberforce's close-knit community was a group of reformers and their families who were committed to ending slavery and helping each other. They understood the long battle would require more than the strength of their convictions. They knew they would need the encouragement and support of other like-minded people. They worked together, socialized together, and many even lived very near to each other. Through it all, Wilberforce and most of his team placed an emphasis on abiding with Christ. This yielding to God's will naturally led them to truly consider the needs of others as more important than themselves.[43] If not for Wilberforce's community of friends, it is likely we would not know his name.

> Unity is the single best way to maintain organizational momentum and accomplish goals.

Just as Wilberforce's successful crusade led to the end the Atlantic slave trade (and eventually slavery in Britain), *organizations powered by unified people can accomplish astounding things.*

Wilberforce's team was unified behind the *why* of their cause: that all human beings were God's children and deserved to be treated well. Each member of the team then concentrated on the *what*, united toward the same goal. Their unified team was unstoppable, prevailing against the entrenched economic and political interests of multiple countries, massive business interests, and millennia of human history.

Wilberforce wasn't a lone wolf. He didn't abolish the Atlantic slave trade by himself.[44] Rather, as a transformational leader, he forged and preserved team unity.

Leaders who abide with Christ and commit to self-leadership, conflict resolution, and healthy workplace relationships also prioritize team unity. Unity is the single best way to maintain organizational momentum and accomplish goals. It makes decisions clearer, and appropriate actions stem from those decisions.

When a husband and wife are not unified because of a conflict, they can do very little as a family. It's as if they are in a foxhole together, facing a common enemy, yet are stealing each other's ammunition. Once they unify, however, they can move forward together. As the African proverb goes, "To run fast, run alone; to run far, run together."

Jesus captured this truth when He said, "Every kingdom divided against itself is laid waste, and no city or house divided against itself will stand" (Matt. 12:25).

Biblical Unity

Transformative and lasting unity rests on a biblical foundation.

Unity is a key concept in Scripture, especially in the New Testament. In the Old Testament, the unity of *God* is stressed. Deuteronomy 6:4, a passage known as the *Shema*, says, "Hear, O Israel: The LORD is our God, the LORD is one," which the

---

44 ???

Israelites used as a confession of faith in the one true God, over and against the competing "gods" of the surrounding nations. King David wrote a song, Psalm 133, that declares, "How good and pleasant it is when brothers dwell in unity!" (v. 1).

In the New Testament, unity among believers was critical as the Christian church began to spread around the world after Pentecost, as recorded in Acts. Paul made this explicit in Galatians 3:28, "There is neither Jew nor Greek, there is neither slave nor free, there is no male and female, for you are all one in Christ Jesus." That unity was vital if the growing church, made up of incredibly diverse people, was to maintain its identity as the body of Christ.

When Jesus returned to His Father, He told the disciples He would send them a helper—the Holy Spirit.[45] The Holy Spirit has always unified the church, and we continue to see this in our day. Christian churches do not need to agree on literally everything, *but they need to be of the same mind, maintaining the unity of the Spirit in the bond of peace.*[46]

Scripture makes it clear that such unity ought to be the default status of believers who are the church. This is the consistent challenge from the writers of the New Testament.

> For as in one body we have many members, and
> the members do not all have the same function,
> so we, though many, are one body in Christ,
> and individually members one of another.
> (Rom. 12:4–5)

> Now there are varieties of gifts, but the same
> Spirit; and there are varieties of service, but the

---

45 See John 14.
46 See 1 Cor. 1:10; Eph. 4:1–6.

same Lord; and there are varieties of activities,
but it is the same God who empowers them all
in everyone. ...For the body does not consist
of one member but of many. If the foot should
say, "Because I am not a hand, I do not belong
to the body," that would not make it any less
a part of the body. And if the ear should say,
"Because I am not an eye, I do not belong to
the body," that would not make it any less a
part of the body. (1 Cor. 12:4–6, 14–16)

I therefore, a prisoner for the Lord, urge you to
walk in a manner worthy of the calling to which
you have been called, with all humility and gentleness, with patience, bearing with one another
in love, eager to maintain the unity of the Spirit
in the bond of peace. There is one body and one
Spirit—just as you were called to the one hope
that belongs to your call—one Lord, one faith,
one baptism. (Eph. 4:1–6)

And above all these put on love, which binds
everything together in perfect harmony.
(Col. 3:14)

Organizational unity is built on these same principles.
Though team members have different functions, and differ
in strengths and weaknesses, they make up one united body.
One department or individual needs the others to be fully
effective.

Just as leaders can destroy unity, leaders who abide in
Christ can model and encourage unity that will transform

their organizations. They can instill their entire team with hope and harmony.

Unity Above All Else

We admit that working in isolation can be appealing.

When no one is challenging you, or suggesting you are wrong, decisions seem clear. The path forward seems self-evident. You get exactly what you want, and every idea sounds like a good one.

And that is precisely the problem: *an organization cannot thrive and remain on mission if its leaders are isolated from one another.*

Romans 12:16 tells us, "Live in harmony with one another. Do not be haughty, but associate with the lowly. Never be wise in your own sight." The leadership lesson there is critical. When you lead an organization from solitude and isolation, you will never do better than so-called "wisdom" in your *own* sight. Working with and through a unified team helps to refine and develop ideas.

Leaders still require "unstructured thinking" or creative time. Both of us cherish quiet times of writing, reading, thinking, praying, listening to music, working out, and even sleeping. (Yes, we even consider sleeping an activity, because good ideas happen while you sleep.) Unstructured time supports creative thinking and provides refreshment and energy. Such times are useful and even necessary to recharge, or "sharpen the saw."

However, solo times cannot be the primary foundation for leadership. Focusing too much on your own preferences and private activities shuts out your team—and that shuts them down. Instead, invite your team into the process, and as a result you will build and maintain team unity—and be better together.

When team members enter a meeting with the expectation of being handed a predetermined to-do list, they become little more than mindless minions. They may very well accomplish their assigned tasks with excellence, but they will not feel like they are a valued part of a team or that they have a stake in the mission.

Such an approach is indicative of leaders who are self-centered and shortsighted. Transformational leaders *want* to incorporate their teams into the process, from start to finish, because they understand that great things will happen. Consider the following progression.

1. Teams who are part of the process spend significant time together.

2. Spending intentional time engaging together creates healthy workplace relationships.

3. Healthy relationships produce ideas that can be refined, tested, and molded into something better or discarded.

4. Team members are encouraged when they are empowered and their contributions are valued.

5. Leaders become more approachable and relatable because team members have been invited into the thought process, and not just asked to execute.

6. The team becomes stronger and more agile—able to respond quickly to change and get better results.

The preferred style of many leaders is to go it alone, come up with ideas, and then watch their team fall in line. But team unity is more important than the preferences of any leader, no matter how visionary. "Isolation is the garden in which idiosyncrasies grow."[47] Idiosyncrasies are "unbecoming quirks." What leader wants to grow into an unbecoming quirk? It doesn't happen on purpose. It is simply the path of least resistance. Spending time together requires leaders who are willing to the take initiative and battle against the current. Unity must be fought for.

Team unity is more important than the preferences of any leader, no matter how visionary.

Wolf packs serve as an illustration of team unity. Despite the rigid role-structure suggested by the familiar term "alpha wolf," the reality is that the pack operates in a loose hierarchy, with different members contributing different skills and strengths at different times, according to their roles. Decisions about hunting are made by the pack, so that any decision with life-or-death consequences has unified buy-in and thus a higher likelihood of success.

In fact, when a "lone wolf" decides to attack *without* buy-in from the pack, even if that wolf is the strongest, he is far more likely to be killed.

It is the same way in an organization. Leaders cannot move forward as lone wolves. Not only will their team suffer, but their own decision-making and results will likely suffer as well.

As tempting as it can be for leaders to go it alone, when leaders place team unity above all else, their organizations will rarely go wrong.

Unity Does Not Mean Unanimity

We will not agree all the time—and that's okay. Too *much* agreement is actually a sign of organizational *sickness*.

47 Todd Wagner, Watermark Church.

Disagreement, shared in healthy and productive ways, is necessary within a thriving organization. In the context of healthy tension, recall these verses:

- Iron sharpens iron, and one man sharpens another. (Prov. 27:17)
- A friend loves at all times, and a brother is born for adversity. (Prov. 17:17)
- Faithful are the wounds of a friend; profuse are the kisses of an enemy. (Prov. 27:6)

These truths were penned by King Solomon, a ruler of unmatched power and wisdom—and someone who had many reasons to justify isolation. Solomon was the most powerful ruler in the world when he wrote these words, yet with the wisdom of God he understood that even kings needed to hear honest feedback from trusted advisors.

Great teams approach problems from different angles. Healthy disagreement provides the opportunity to test and refine the discussion, and unity *without* discussion and disagreement is unity in name only.

Clear organizational roles and multiple levels of decision making remain critical for the organization. Just as the executive team does not need to weigh in on snacks for the break room, neither does the client services team need to pitch in ideas for GAAP accounting best practices. However, clear communication throughout the organization is central to every healthy organization.

Effective leaders know the fruit of healthy disagreement is unity. Don't be tempted to settle for halfhearted consensus and think you've created unity.

Destroying Unity Is Easy, but Rebuilding It Takes Time

Unfortunately, unity is easy to destroy and difficult to rebuild.

It is a mistake to consider your team's emotions and energy level as "optional" or something to consider only *after* all the work is accomplished. The reality of life in any organization is that there will be seasons of discouragement. These could be as short as an interaction with an irate client, or as lengthy as a discussion about compensation or roles over time.

It is natural for team members to beat themselves up when something perceived as negative happens—and leaders can be the worst at such self-criticism. Despite knowing that our overall lives are contributing value to our organizations, we can find ourselves pondering thoughts destructive to our well-being. We can focus on how we have fallen short or missed a goal, to the exclusion of our positive contributions.

The "emotional bank account" of your team can be drained all too easily. In the presence of discouraging events, or even in the absence of encouragement, the unity you've worked so hard to build can dissolve. When a deadline is looming and your team is working late, the unity you've worked so hard to build can be endangered by something as simple as a careless comment or thoughtless grumbling.

One example of behavior that destroys unity is bringing up a past disagreement *after* a path forward has already been chosen. It is understandably tempting to dwell on past mistakes. However, "being right" and letting others know about it destroys unity for the sake of selfish pride. It might feel good for a moment, but an approach like this ruins what you are working so hard to build. Leaders get the organizations they deserve—so if an "I told you so" culture is what you want, all you have to do is model it. Such disunity will ripple outward from the leadership and across the entire organization.

Other ways that unity can be destroyed include:

- Any behavior inconsistent with the values of the organization that isn't dealt with and reconciled
- Recurring competency issues that are not dealt with openly or quickly
- A lack of chemistry between two team members and an unwillingness to acknowledge the issue and deal with it
- Over-controlling preferences from a leader that prevent team members from leading their respective areas of responsibility
- An unwillingness to deal with a lingering issue or challenge that is hindering the business

And this list could be much longer. We all know how easily true unity can be undermined and destroyed by even minor choices. Fortunately, when unity is destroyed, it *can* be built back up. But it takes time and consistent effort.

As Mark Twain once quipped, "Trust leaves on horseback but returns on foot," and that applies equally to unity. There are several ways by which leaders can restore broken unity in an organization, but it is always built on the foundation of humility. We saw in chapter 2 that a biblical, transformational leader is, first and foremost, a *servant* leader.

Unity requires a tremendous amount of humility from leaders. Just as leaders need the humility not to "go it alone," so too leaders need the humility to place the needs of others ahead of their own. If team members sense that a leader truly has their best interests in mind, they will unify behind that leader. And the unity will be contagious, because a unified team will *also* place the needs of others ahead of their own.

It is possible to cultivate and maintain a corporate culture in which unity and selflessness "go viral." But it is hard.

One of Matt's mentors, Kyle (different than the Kyle we mentioned in chapter 3), is a clear example of this. He is never too busy to pick up the phone or meet for coffee. He treats his time as if it belongs to others, and when others call on him, he uses the opportunity to encourage them. And he is consistently kind, rather than harsh and critical. When he needs to speak a hard truth, he does so out of love. Because of his deep personal walk with the Lord and his outlook of believing the best about others, his counsel can be trusted.

This selfless investment carries over outside the boundaries of the workplace. He may exercise with a team member, or invite someone over to share a meal with his family.

Sadly, there are some, especially in the business world, who would consider Kyle "weak." They would believe he gives too much away for free. That he fails to leverage the respect people have for him into economic or relational advantage.

Such opinions could not be more wrong. The opposite is true, in fact. Kyle, *because of his consistent servanthood and humility, is an instrument of grace to his friends and helps them work toward great things.* So many who are effectively serving others in our community were directly inspired and equipped by the way Kyle invested in them.

Transformational leaders must seek to be more like Kyle. Such an approach to work and life benefits everyone in the organization, as well as countless lives beyond the organization.

Once a leader has established a culture of humility, a culture of encouragement can follow. Just as discouragement destroys unity, encouragement strengthens it. Yet it is not simply the reverse process. In our experience, it takes much longer to build unity with encouragement than it does to destroy it. Think of a section of forest leveled in a single day by wildfire—it will take far longer for the trees to return to their former height.

James, the half-brother of Jesus, offers a sober reminder of the power of a discouraging word: "So also the tongue is a small member, yet it boasts of great things. How great a forest is set ablaze by such a small fire! And the tongue is a fire, a world of unrighteousness. The tongue is set among our members, staining the whole body" (James 3:5–6). Proverbs 18:21 tells us that our words can bring life or death. Leaders must intentionally consider everything they say and ask themselves, "Will what I'm about to say bring life, encouragement, and unity? Or will it bring discouragement, distrust, and disunity?"

One of the best ways to create a unified team is to make a habit of encouraging your team and providing them opportunities to encourage each other. An encouraging word falls on the soul like rain on a desert. Often it's desperately needed. Try employing the metric of encouragement to yourself and your team as a way to evaluate health.

- How many of your team members are encouragers?
- How many of your managers are encouragers?
- How often are *you* encouraging others?
- What habits could you develop to increase the amount of encouragement?

Making deposits into the emotional bank account of your team paves the way for great conversations, lightens their burdens as they move forward, and brings people together in unity.

The Power of Unity

Long before power tools and towering cranes capable of lifting steel girders, cathedrals were constructed over the course of long, back-breaking decades. Every element of the cathedral had to be created by hand, from the wooden pews to the colorful stained glass to the massive stone walls. Whole towns developed around the construction site, and workers could expect to spend their entire lives laboring on that single project.

Now imagine you are a traveler, stepping across the muddy ground of such a work site. The first buttresses are beginning to creep toward the sky, foot by foot, piece by piece. Everything around you is humming with activity. Workers scramble across the yard, dragging timber and blocks of quarried stone. It is likely that some of the workers will never even live to see the cathedral completed, or sit in one of the pews to worship.

You near a row of masons. Others have dropped off a rough chunk of white stone in front of each mason, and each mason leans over his stone, chisel in one hand and hammer in the other. Their powerful arms rise, fall, and another small fleck of stone is removed in just the right spot. Blow by blow, the rough cubic blocks are being shaped into precise pieces.

You step close to the first man and ask, between his hammer strokes, "What are you doing, friend?"

He looks at you strangely, as if you'd asked whether water was wet. "Cutting stone," he says brusquely, returning to his labor.

Continuing down the line, you ask the same question of the second man. He gestures with his head toward one of the nearby foundations, from which the lower reaches of a wall have begun to protrude. "Making blocks for a window arch," he says.

The window arch will be capable of bearing enormous weight, and it will contain one of the many colored windows depicting scenes from the Bible. His pieces will be combined with the products of other workers, creating a unified whole. You can almost picture the rainbow light slanting through the finished creation.

Having received such different answers from the first two workers, you approach the third man and ask him the same question.

Setting his hammer down atop the block of stone, he wipes the sweat from his head with his forearm. "Well now," he ponders, letting his practiced eyes roam across the yard, taking in the myriad details, before coming back to rest on his block of stone. Unaccountably, a grin cracks his weathered face, and he takes his hammer back into his hand.

"We're building a cathedral."[48]

◆

Which man is best suited to represent the vision behind the construction? The one who sees only his "job"? The one who sees only his stone and the stone's next use? Or the one who understands the greater task that unifies all their labor?

Each mason was performing the same task, but each mason was approaching that task with a different mindset.

The first man was a "clock puncher," working only for a paycheck. He had no sense that he was part of anything bigger or more significant than what was directly in front of his nose. If another offer came along with better wages, he'd be likely to jump at it.

---

48 This is our version of a common teaching story that can be found in many places.

The second man was a "team player." He knew the connection between what he was doing and the next step of the process. But he lacked a full understanding of the meaning of his work, and the importance of his place on the team.

The third man, however, was a "stakeholder in the vision" who truly understood what his work meant. Over the years he would certainly have disagreements with his foreman or other workers. He would go through ups and downs. But through it all, he would keep his sense of his larger *mission and his place in it.*

> It isn't your responsibility as a leader to have an ideal organization. But you must have a *mission* worth fighting for.

When it comes to your team, a mission-mindset matters. People want to be part of something vastly larger than themselves. Something inspiring. Something that is making a difference in the world. *Unity around mission is what transforms mere blocks of stones into cathedrals.*

It isn't your responsibility as a leader to have an ideal organization. But you must have a *mission* worth fighting for. Consider what defines you, and the reason for your existence.

- Do you view your business as something more than a profit generator?
- Does your product or service improve people's lives?
- Long after you are gone, will others take up the leadership of your organization because of its compelling vision and value to the community?

Clear, biblical answers to these questions put you and your organization on the path to unity.

Just as conflict resolution is the most valuable single skill for a leader, unity is the most valuable asset of a team. A unified team will maintain momentum and accomplish goals. Cultivate a team of "cathedral builders" who do more than just get work done—they understand the vision, the mission, and the unique value they are contributing toward it.

A unified leadership team will accomplish amazing things together. William Wilberforce and his team changed the world forever. You and your team can too.

Discussion Questions:

1. Is your organization characterized by unity across various levels?

2. How do the Scriptures we shared about biblical unity (Rom. 12:4–5; 1 Cor. 12:4–6, 14–16; Eph. 4:1–6; Col. 3:14) apply to your organization?

3. What lessons about leadership do you draw from the behavior of wolf packs?

4. Can you think of a time when your team enjoyed unity without unanimity?

5. Are you guilty of tearing down unity? If so, what positive behaviors can you choose to slowly build it back up?

6. How can your organization begin to see itself as working together to build something bigger?

"I in them and you in me, that they may become
perfectly one, so that the world may know
that you sent me and loved them
even as you loved me." (John 17:23)

Chapter Seven

GENEROSITY

No Better Investment

Courageous leadership defines great organizations—and generosity requires great courage.

Ambrose Redmoon's definition of courage is telling: "Courage is not the absence of fear, but rather the judgment that something else is more important than fear."[49] Generosity begins when leaders make it a habit to boldly invest in those around them, trusting that it will produce positive results.

> Godly generosity expects nothing in return, yet the return on generosity is beyond measure.

Generosity is the quality of being kind, understanding, and unselfish as you *willingly give to others*. This means choosing to share your possessions, your time, your energy, your skills, and your focus. "Others" may include a close friend, a great employee, a difficult coworker, a frustrating boss, a

---

49 Julia Keller, "The Mysterious Ambrose Redmoon's Healing Words," *Chicago Tribune*, March 29, 2002, http://articles.chicagotribune.com/2002-03-29/ features/0203290018_1_chicago-police-officer-terry-hillard-courage.

distant teenager, an aging father, an ex-spouse, a lonely veteran, an orphaned child, or a single mom.[50]

Godly generosity *expects* nothing in return, yet the *return* on generosity is beyond measure. Transformational leaders invest in generosity because it changes lives. That simple but true statement should be all the motivation we need to be generous.

Deliberately practicing this discipline molds you into a stronger, more resilient, and trustworthy leader. Every new habit requires consistent and unusual amounts of practice and courage, but choosing this path will have a positive, enduring impact on your organization and the people connected to it. Generosity in your organization can be described the same way Peter Drucker describes management: "Its task is to make people capable of joint performance, to make their strengths effective and their weaknesses irrelevant."[51]

When the joy of generosity is discovered it becomes contagious. Consistently practicing generosity models and promotes a relationship-based, others-focused culture across the entire organization.

Consider Andrew, one of Matt's former employees. Soon after he was hired, another employee invited Andrew to volunteer at a local Young Life chapter. (Young Life is a Christian organization that shares God's love with kids). This particular chapter was dedicated to kids with special needs. Andrew agreed, although somewhat reluctantly. He was fresh out of college, starting his career, and trying to find his way in life. Did he have enough free time to be generous? And he'd never worked with special needs kids before, so he

---

50 Matt. 5:43–48.
51 Peter F. Drucker, *The Essential Drucker* (New York: HarperBusiness, 2008).

wasn't sure what he could offer them. Still, he decided to give it a try. Some of his fellow employees volunteered outside of work, and it seemed like part of the culture.

One day, about three months later, Andrew walked into Matt's office with tears glistening in his eyes.

"Matt," he asked, "can I give you a hug?"

Matt agreed to what turned out to be a bear hug. As Andrew stepped back, Matt asked Andrew what was going on.

"Getting to work alongside these kids has changed my life."

A seasoned employee invested in Andrew when he was first hired. Then when Andrew invested in his community, he became a better employee *and* a better person. Now his generosity will continue to bear fruit as he makes a positive impact in the lives of others.

Andrew had something more than tears shining in his eyes that day. He was feeling *joy*. Andrew had discovered firsthand what everyone who has had the privilege of investing generously in others knows: "Whoever brings blessing will be enriched, and one who waters will himself be watered" (Prov. 11:25).

Such generosity may require taking a risk, but it need not be a dramatic one. Generosity begins small. There are many simple ways to be generous at work. The following list is adapted from Jodi Glickman,[52] and it is far from exhaustive. Each item can include myriad specific examples. Consider how each of these could be pursued daily, in fresh ways, over the course of an entire career.

- Look for specific ways to serve your boss, colleagues, and team.

---

52 Jodi Glickman, "Be Generous At Work," Harvard Business Review, June 8, 2011, https://hbr.org/2011/06/be-generous-at-work.

- Think about what your boss and teammates will need next.
- Share information quickly, accurately, fully, and clearly.
- Ask if someone has a few minutes to talk before starting a conversation.
- Share credit and compliments.
- Give your time and experience as a mentor.

All of these are generous acts because they demonstrate the value of the other person, even at the cost of personal convenience.

The generous culture created by such actions can produce generous organizations, and people will take notice. Many organizations are using generosity strategies to build positive relationships, according to Eddie Yoon, including TD Bank providing free coin changers, Costco providing free samples, and Netflix providing free month-long trials and releasing shows all at once instead of week-by-week.[53] Such actions, he writes, generate "positive PR buzz and goodwill among customers"—for example, less than *1 percent* of the people who signed up for Netflix's free trial quit the service when the month was up. Yoon suggests another way of evaluating the effectiveness of generosity is to consider its opposite: *stinginess* is not a quality any organization, or any individual, should aspire to.

We love that Yoon points out the "root of generosity is the same as genesis, genius, and generate." Doesn't that sound like the kind of organization you'd like to be part of?

---

53 Eddie Yoon, "The Generosity Strategies That Help Companies Grow," *Harvard Business Review*, May 2, 2013, https://hbr.org/2013/05/netflix-reported-another-great.

Our Greatest Reward

Perhaps the question remains, however: Is being generous *truly* a core organizational need, or is it more of a beneficial add-on?

Here is a compelling answer from Jeff's experience. It demonstrates that if you are generous in your work life—not simply in your free time—it will absolutely lead to positive impact, both in your work life *and* your personal life.

Imagine growing up in some of the roughest neighborhoods in America. Imagine getting married while you're still a teenager, then having an autistic and epileptic son, followed by a divorce. Imagine being industrious and hard-working, but with no strong parental guidance and no positive choices, making a living by running several night clubs and hiring guys to sell drugs for you on the side.

Now imagine getting arrested on drug charges and looking at up to ninety-nine hopeless years in jail.

But then imagine a guy in jail introduces you to someone named Jesus, and your life is transformed. Imagine a sympathetic judge grants you early parole. Imagine finding yourself free, a new believer, but living back in the same neighborhood that got you into jail in the first place, with no family, no positive friends, and no support system. You can make a lot of money quickly, just like the old days, but that's not who you are anymore. You can live at a shelter indefinitely, but you don't want to get comfortable there. You want to grow in your faith, and find honest work, and put the pieces of your life back together.

You try to connect at nearby churches, but all you receive are quick prayers and pats on the back. You're on the verge of turning your life around, but you can't get there by yourself—you're living on the floor of an abandoned warehouse and you could easily fall back into your criminal past. Imagine the *one* thing that would make a real difference in your life.

Generosity. *True* generosity. Generosity that gives you what you need most: encouragement, advice, a relationship, trust. And most of all, generosity that gives you a chance.

This is actually the story of a real man named Carlos.[54] Jeff first met him after he made his way to church and filled out a card, asking for help. Jeff called Carlos and heard his story and suggested a meeting. They met at a local McDonald's and began a relationship. Jeff was able to ask Carlos what would make the biggest tangible impact on his difficult life, and Carlos knew the answer.

"I get fired from any job as soon as they find out about my record. I need someone who *knows* about my record to give me a shot. I'll work for free for a week to prove myself!"

Three weeks later, during which time Jeff continued to meet with Carlos to study the Bible and pray and talk, Jeff offered to sponsor Carlos in the Faith at Work program. This is an initiative at Jeff and Matt's church that matches employers in the church body with people in discipling relationships who have barriers to traditional employment, such as people who are homeless or formerly incarcerated. Each applicant has a church sponsor who coaches them and helps to bridge the employer-employee relationship. The church also teaches courses on biblical financial stewardship and some soft skills training.

Now fast-forward to the time of this writing. Carlos has experienced many good things. He's been growing spiritually, and he was able to find work at a company owned by a member of the church. He has saved some money, paid off fines related

---

54 We have changed his name to protect his identity.

to his incarceration, and secured his own apartment. He is excited to be able to financially provide for his son and has taken steps to reconnect with his ex-wife. He's reaching out to other homeless or struggling men he knows, telling them about the generous God who loves them.

He has also experienced some down times, such as being fired from his job and feeling discouraged. He will bounce back, we believe, but it is likely he will continue to experience ups and downs on his journey, just like the rest of us.

God does not invite us to invest in others because it will guarantee a certain outcome. Rather, we invest generously in others because it gives them the opportunity to follow God more fully. After all, God invests in *us* yet still gives us freedom.

The bottom line is Carlos is being used by God. His life testifies to the will and work of God, through God's generous people. Think about the key figures whose generosity gave Carlos a chance for a new life that can make a positive impact: the man who shared the gospel with him in jail, the kind judge, Jeff and his ministry team, the business owner who took a chance on Carlos. All of these people invested in his life, and now Carlos can invest in the lives of others.

We don't know the end of Carlos's story yet, but we hope one day, in God's grace, to look back at a life transformed by God in order to transform others. From individual lives, the impact of generosity spreads across entire organizations... and beyond.

How *Not* to Be Generous

Generosity is an essential outgrowth of healthy leadership, and it is one of the best investments imaginable.

However, there *are* wrong ways to practice it. A corporate day of service or undertaking certain community projects does not guarantee impact or effectiveness. Unless the effort aligns with the mission and purpose of your organization, there is a very real chance you will be generating nothing more than "busy work" for your employees. In fact, helping can actually hurt in ways that might not be initially obvious.

For example, we know of a church that was periodically sending teams into a run-down, urban neighborhood to do rehab work on a large, deteriorating house. When the teams came back they would report what a wonderful time they had serving and "making a difference." They were motivated by the admirable desire to be generous in their community. One day, however, the church learned something disturbing from someone who lived very near to the house that was being renovated: "You guys made the nicest looking crack house in the city!"

The revelation was disheartening, but ultimately made the church wiser about how to practice their generosity. With that in mind, the following three principles can help steer us away from unwise generosity.

Don't give blindly.

Being more generous does not necessarily mean that you should give away more money.

It is tempting, for organizations as well as individuals, to simply budget a greater amount of money for charitable giving. Sometimes writing a check to a nonprofit is the right answer, especially if your organization is working with a trusted community partner with whom you have interacted successfully in the past. Money can be part of an effective solution.

However, we can make the mistake of assuming that money is the primary solution. Giving money to a community organization may salve your conscience, but it may not lead to lasting change.

Rather than blindly giving "treasure" away, we need to be wise. As the Bible instructs us in Psalm 41, we are to consider the poor. (And this can include all types of poverty: physical, emotional, spiritual, and so on.) That means we need to bring to bear the same creativity and acumen we'd apply to a problem at work.

Bob Lupton, a believer who focuses on Christian community development in Atlanta, said it provocatively: "Charity can be the kindest way to kill someone." Unfortunately, when we "give" we may actually be taking. Our well-intentioned but misplaced generosity may be taking away people's dignity, value, worth, and inherent desire for productivity and work.

Take the example of funding a new cement mixer for a local builder in Uganda. It is possible such a gift might steal jobs from locals who used to do that job manually. These consequences are unintentional, of course, but they are still real.

The reality is that blindly giving money away can be a one-way resource dump. In our desire to be generous, we can give people money or resources, and we may not have really *given* them anything.

Don't mistake activity for impact.

Second, even when blind giving isn't an issue, many organizations and individuals view *activity* as the goal, rather than *impact*.

When we are active in giving or volunteering, we nearly always *feel* productive. Yet sometimes activity is best described in the famous words of Shakespeare's *Macbeth*: "full of sound and fury, signifying nothing" (Act 5, Scene 5).

For example, Jeff's church used to have an annual "service weekend." Sunday services were cancelled, and everyone hopped on over fifty school busses and drove all over the city. They had a list of projects designed to improve the community. Painting lockers in schools, weeding flowerbeds in parks, doing light construction…the list went on and on.

The trouble is, despite the good intentions, the service weekend created many more problems than it solved.

- The church's ministry partners in the community were stretched to the breaking point. Typically, they were stretched already, as most nonprofits are. But having to come up with what amounted primarily to "busy work" for hundreds of volunteers drained their resources even further.
- It cost the missions team at church months of planning that could have been better spent on other projects.

- It failed to effectively connect the members'
  hearts and skill sets with opportunities to
  engage and serve. For example, if a banker
  is asked to pass out snow cones (rather than
  to help set up an LLC for a new job-train-
  ing initiative), the expected level of passion
  and excitement is very low.
- Finally, it didn't last longer than a weekend
  because very few real relationships were
  built. It was a "one-and-done" event.

Ultimately the church realized that such
activity amounted to a one-way chance for
them to "give," but with little lasting impact.

God isn't calling us to generous "busy work,"
but rather to generous *impact*. The church has
since moved to service opportunities that are
more targeted, and on a smaller scale, so that
people from the church can join ministry partners strategically and build real, lasting relationships with those they are serving alongside.

Our organizations can make similar mistakes. We need to eliminate activity for the sake
of activity, and focus our generosity on making a
tangible difference in the lives of real people.

Don't confuse a chronic problem with a crisis.
Third, there are two kinds of problems in our
communities: crisis and chronic.[55]

---

55 For additional information on the stages of development, see Robert
Lupton, *Toxic Charity: How Churches and Charities Hurt Those They
Help (and How to Reverse It)* (New York: HarperOne, 2011) and

Crisis problems require relief and resources, such as when a tornado destroys parts of a town's infrastructure. Chronic problems, on the other hand, require long-term solutions. We would criticize a doctor who provided only painkillers to a patient without attempting to cure the disease causing the pain. Yet our efforts to be generous can have the same effect.

Is it wrong to serve meals to the homeless? Certainly not! The Bible tells us that the fruit of the Spirit is love, joy, peace, patience, kindness, goodness, faithfulness, gentleness, and self-control, and it's never wrong to demonstrate these qualities. But we cannot be satisfied with only crisis relief. For example, when evaluating their ministry to the homeless, Jeff's church likes to ask the question, "How many people did we move out of homelessness and into discipleship-based jobs this month?" The ultimate goal of that ministry is to work itself out of existence.

What you believe about the *cause* of an issue will influence how you believe it should be solved. When the only option for generosity we give ourselves is "writing a check" or "serving soup at a shelter," we are missing out on hearing from people who may be the greatest source of problem-solving wisdom. The people you want to serve are, in all likelihood, the same people

Steve Corbett and Brian Fikkert, *When Helping Hurts: How to Alleviate Poverty without Hurting the Poor... and Yourself* (Chicago, IL: Moody Publishers, 2009).

who know many of the answers to their problems. *What they lack is the capacity to make those
answers happen.*

You've heard the expression, "God helps
those who help themselves." The reality is that
God helps *all* of us. The Bible tells us that God
gives natural resources and common grace to
all. In fact, we are instructed to use whatever
gifts we have received to serve others, as faithful stewards of God's grace in its various forms
(1 Pet. 4:10). Perhaps we should change the
expression to, "God helps *all* of us so we can
help each other."

These three cautionary points are not intended to scare us
away from generosity, but rather to steer us toward the right
kind of generosity: the kind that makes a positive and lasting
difference in the lives of everyone involved.

Numbering Our Days

Ironically, the more generous we are, the more time we
may find for what really matters.

Those oriented toward achievement can easily drift into
valuing the product over people. The task or goal can, at times,
become more important than people. We know intellectually
this is not true, but practically we can find ourselves working this way. Healthy lead-
ers must continually reaffirm
their purpose. Focus allows us
to say no to the less important
task and yes to people more
often. Great companies are

**Trusting God with time
can be one of the most generous
things you can do.**

built on great people. And great leaders consistently invest in the most important part of their business: their people.

The more we attempt to control people or circumstances, the more anxious we can become. Instead, the Bible encourages us to "number our days," and when the Bible gives us a *what*, there is also a *why*: "that we may gain a heart of wisdom."

There are laws of arithmetic to biblical timekeeping, and God must tutor us in them. As God teaches us to number our days, we gain wisdom and learn to follow Him more effectively.

What opportunities should we choose? What should we refuse? What is the best way to order our day, week, quarter, and year? For example, interruptions can seem inconvenient until we learn what Henri Nouwen did when he exclaimed, "My whole life I have been complaining that my work was constantly interrupted, until I discovered the interruptions were my work."

The Bible teaches us that God is in control of our days and years. God's thoughts are not our thoughts, neither are our ways His ways.[56] God's purposes and presence often come disguised as detours, distractions, and even defeats. Consider the events in your life that have shaped you the most profoundly. How many did you see coming? How many did you engineer or plan? And how many were surprises?

When we treat time as though it belongs to God (because it does), and give it away generously, we discover that we have all the time we need to do the work He has prepared in advance for us to do.[57] However, when we guard the moments, even if our reasons seem good, we will never have enough time. Trusting God with time can be one of the most generous things you can do.

---

56 Isa. 55:8.
57 Eph. 2:10.

Even so, generosity *is* an investment, and like all investments, it needs to be evaluated.

Leaders must apply prudence and wisdom before giving. Leaders must be honest about what is working and what isn't. If something isn't working, we must be willing to deal openly with the facts and address the issue with those involved.[58]

Any step toward generosity is a good first step. It takes the focus off of self and puts it onto others. What we are advocating is wisdom and prudence in the process for the purpose of improving our generosity.

For example, if we were evaluating a marketing investment for our business, we would examine the opportunity and ask questions like:

- How much money will we be spending, and over what length of time?
- What do we expect the firm will receive from the investment?
- Will the investment produce new client leads?
- Will the investment generate revenue?
- Will it have a positive impact on firm reputation?

If the investment is unlikely to generate the return we are seeking, we would not pursue it. *We need to evaluate our generosity with the same level of thoughtfulness.*

At a high level, take a moment and think through your kingdom-related investments:

---

58 Matt. 7:3–5.

Investment Category	Investment of Time, Talent or Treasure?	Working or Not?	What Needs to Change?	Next Steps?
Family				
Work				
Church				

Consider discussing what you discover with your spouse, business partners, ministry partners, and close friends. Community can be very helpful as we consider changes to our generosity, since nearly every idea we have in isolation sounds like a good one. "Without counsel plans fail, but with many advisers they succeed" (Prov. 15:22).

As you refine and discover what you want to accomplish through generosity, you will be able to quickly sift through opportunities and articulate why you chose to do X and not Y. You will also be better able to communicate with others who may want to help and enlist their support.

The challenges facing our communities are many: lack of educational opportunity, scarce access to affordable housing, appropriate job creation, and so on. But the *opportunity* to develop, evaluate, and implement ideas that have both an immediate and an eternal impact exist. When leaders provide their employees the chance to use their God-given talents and passions in service of others, their enthusiasm and energy levels will encourage those watching to do likewise.

We tend to be most excited to use our specific gifts in tangible kingdom-advancing ways. That isn't to say we can't learn new things or serve outside our comfort zones. Sometimes we discover new areas where we can make a difference.

> We serve a God who is infinitely generous with us, and we are called to courageously extend that generosity to others.

When we bring people together to be generous *inside their area of passion and expertise,* however, it will often have an impact that far exceeds initial expectations, both within and outside our organizations.

Adam Grant summarizes the organizational value of generosity in the article "In the Company of Givers and Takers" (*emphasis added*).

> Organizations have a strong interest in fostering giving behavior. A willingness to help others achieve their goals lies at the heart of effective collaboration, innovation, quality improvement, and service excellence. In workplaces where such behavior becomes the norm, the benefits multiply quickly. Consider a landmark meta-analysis led by Nathan Podsakoff, of the University of Arizona. His team examined 38 studies of organizational behavior, representing more than 3,500 business units and many different industries, and found that *the link between employee giving and desirable business outcomes was surprisingly robust. Higher rates of giving were predictive of higher unit profitability, productivity, efficiency, and customer*

satisfaction, along with lower costs and turnover
rates. When employees act like givers, they facili-
tate efficient problem solving and coordination and
build cohesive, supportive cultures that appeal to
customers, suppliers, and top talent alike.[59]

That is why generosity is vital to healthy leadership and
flourishing organizations. We serve a God who is infinitely
generous with us, and we are called to courageously extend
that generosity to others.

---

59 Adam Grant, "In the Company of Givers and Takers," *Har-vard Business Review*, April 2013, https://hbr.org/2013/04/
in-the-company-of-givers-and-takers.

Discussion Questions:

1. Does generosity seem like an investment to you, or more like an optional cost?

2. What are some specific ways you practice generosity in your organization?

3. Are you guilty of being "generous" in the wrong ways discussed in this chapter?

4. What does God's sovereign control over our time mean for the way you spend your days?

"Whoever brings blessing will be enriched,
and one who waters will himself be watered."
(Prov. 11:25)

Chapter Eight

MENTORSHIP AND DISCIPLESHIP

Choosing Guides

The best investment in another person is mentorship.

"Mentor" is a character in Homer's *Odyssey* who advises the young Telemachus when he is faced with difficult choices. In the context of modern business (and life), mentors do the same thing: provide wise, trusted counsel. A true mentor invests in a relationship over time, contextually modeling wise choices. A mentor doesn't just say the right things, but "walks the talk."

Surprisingly, this is a mutually beneficial relationship. Because of the relationship with the mentee, the mentor is encouraged to be more honest, self-reflective, and purposeful, so both people grow and mature.

Ken Perlman, writing for Kotter International, says it this way: "The value of a mentor who can help cultivate leadership skills one-on-one in real-time, reduce the anxiety in taking big steps, and focus leaders on achieving their goals—is huge."[60]

Indeed, mentorship has a positive effect on every stage of an employee's time with an organization. The sort of meaningful

---

60 Ken Perlman, Kotter International, "The Often Overlooked but Invaluable Benefits of Mentorship," *Forbes*, January 30,2013, http://www.forbes.com/sites/johnkotter/2013/01/30/the-often-overlooked-but-invaluable-benefits-of-mentorship/.

relationships that can be built through mentorship will help any organization attract, develop, and ultimately retain top talent, as well as develop top talent into mentors themselves. Ask healthy leaders how they got to where they are now, and business mentorship will be one of the first answers. When someone takes the time to slow down and invest in your life, it pays huge dividends and makes it natural for *you* to want to invest in others as well.

There is no fixed progression that a mentor/mentee relationship must go through, but there are common positive impacts. Confidence and skills can be gained. Encouragement can be given. Mentors can act as a sounding board for new hires. Lasting friendships can be built. Crises can be navigated successfully.

However, the concept of apprenticeship provides a useful way to think about the steps most mentor/mentee relationships follow. Apprenticeship has been for centuries the primary method for equipping generations of workers with on-the-job training. Whether you were a mason, a baker, or even a knight, you learned to effectively practice your craft through placing yourself under the leadership of a skilled craftsman.

An apprentice begins by working alongside his or her master, gradually gaining knowledge and skill. Journeymen have measurable competencies, but not yet the extensive experience to work alone or mentor others. And masters, while continuing to learn, possess both the necessary skill and the wisdom to apply and teach it.

An oft-cited way of describing that progression—and picturing mentorship in an organizational context—is this:

> I do, you watch.
> I do, you help.

You do, I help.

You do, I watch.

When any organization has a variety of healthy relationships that are impacting employees at all levels, a final step can be added to that process: *We do together.*

Today the apprentice model still exists, albeit in fewer trades. As a result, we have lost the perspective that *all* of us are apprentices at one time or another. Depending on what you are doing, your role may switch from master to apprentice to journeyman and back again, even in a single day. You can be a general practitioner, with skills across many areas of expertise, or you can be a craftsman focused on a single area of expertise. The opportunities to learn and to teach are everywhere.

These mutually beneficial relationships begin when we avoid the roadblock of fear and live life together. They are sustained, however, when we sit at the feet of Jesus and learn from the Master. Every single day. Healthy leadership begins with self-leadership that is grounded in an abiding relationship with Christ.

> **We cannot impart what we do not possess, and only Jesus possesses all of what we need to lead well.**

We cannot impart what we do not possess, and only Jesus possesses all of what we need to lead well. He is the wisest, kindest, most patient, most driven, most humble, and most honorable leader any of us will ever learn from.

When we are actively learning from Jesus, each day we will discover ways to serve others and look out for their best interest. The payback is enormous, both for our organization and in God's kingdom. When our workplace relationships make us more like Jesus, we cannot help impacting our families and communities.

There are at least four key reasons that mentorship is a powerful and generous investment. [61]

Mentoring gives new hires a head start.

When working in a new organization there is an inevitable learning curve. Every organization has its own way of doing things, but mentorship shortens the learning curve, enabling newer team members to engage quickly.

When seasoned employees serve as a mentor, they help those new to the organization understand the culture and acclimate to their work environment. When a mentor checks in regularly with a new hire during a lengthy and difficult project, they demonstrate through behavior that the new employee is both valuable and important.

In some cases, these relationships develop and deepen over the years, providing ongoing benefits for both people, as well as the organization.

Mentorship clarifies next steps.

Depending on the size of the organization, there is a chance that new hires will be "lost in the shuffle." They show up to work each day and fulfill their job requirements, but the individualized attention that will take that employee to the next level of performance within the organization may be missing.

---

61 Credit to Morgan Eseke for helping to create this content initially.

Mentorship can provide exactly that. The relationship between a mentor and mentee provides an opportunity to discuss the employee's career goals and offer guidance and development opportunities for the mentee. Individualized attention of an employee's key career goals is critical to retaining top talent and ensuring that an individual's unique gifts and passions are fully utilized.

Mentorship is leadership development.

We view the people we work with, at all levels, as leaders. If we didn't, they wouldn't be part of our teams.

To that end, mentorship provides an effective opportunity to develop leadership skills. Mentorship is personal and nonthreatening allowing leadership lessons to be effectively translated. This works in both directions. Mentors often need to fine-tune their management and communication skills while investing in junior employees.

Mentorship is self-development.

Taking your eyes off yourself is one of the most valuable tools for leadership development.

Similar to peer friendships, mentorship is an opportunity to take your eyes off yourself. Both mentor and mentee have the opportunity to support one another through encouraging words, sound advice, or hands-on assistance. Mentors celebrate great wins and encourage mentees when they are struggling. Mentor relationships are fundamentally established with the expectation of personal growth, particularly for the mentee. Mentors and mentees alike have the green light to challenge one another to improve and to pursue excellence at work.

The Fruit of Mentorship Is Discipleship

The value and importance of such mutually beneficial relationships is captured in Ecclesiastes 4:9–10:

> Two are better than one, because they have a good reward for their toil. For if they fall, one will lift up his fellow. But woe to him who is alone when he falls and has not another to lift him up.[62]

On this journey, so much of what we're talking about is discipleship and abiding in Christ. Discipleship is usually talked about in churches, not the business world. However, a disciple is simply someone who is actively learning and growing in the context of a relationship. An organization of discipleship is one in which people are consistently being developed, challenged, and encouraged to become effective leaders who, in turn, can develop others.

Discipleship is transformative. Through God's generous grace, and the generosity of those who are leaders for God, parents are restored

> An organization of discipleship is one in which people are consistently being developed, challenged, and encouraged to become effective leaders who, in turn, can develop others.

---

62 See also Prov. 13:20: "Whoever walks with the wise becomes wise."

to their children. Marriages are reconciled. The dignity of work offers hope to the jobless. Employees see their work as a godly calling and an opportunity to serve and love others. These outcomes literally change the future of households, neighborhoods, and even cities. Godly mentorship *is* discipleship—and nothing impacts individuals or organizations more than discipleship.

Mentors who abide in Christ will:

- Share encouraging and challenging Scripture
- Ask clarifying questions about thoughts and actions
- Value the truth while speaking with gentleness and humility
- Lead by example
- Examine their own lives in light of their relationship with the mentee

Godly mentors understand that discipleship is the ultimate goal of relationships. Why? Because discipleship connects individuals with the bottomless resources of God.

Imagine an investor who says to an entrepreneur, "I don't care how much of my money you spend, as long as you invest it in the priorities we've agreed on. I'm comfortable with you deciding what to do. Let's change the world together."

God wants to give us unlimited startup capital. Second Peter 1:3 says, "His divine power has granted to us all things that pertain to life and godliness, through the knowledge of him who called us to his own glory and excellence." That means that when we walk with Jesus we will be provided with everything required to think and act as God desires.

Knowing that, we would be much more likely to attempt things outside our comfort zones. Let's lead with confidence, knowing our resources belong to God and are replenished by God. If we trust Him, God will use what He has given us to accomplish His good purposes. Let's take stock of the people around us. If our families, employees, and clients are truly flourishing, this will be both our highest goal and our greatest reward.

Discipleship Culture

An organization firing on all cylinders is one characterized by a culture of discipleship. Its leaders understand that in every transaction, discussion, meeting, phone call, decision, or deal, discipleship is occurring.

When leaders and employees are being positively discipled, great things happen. If all other factors are equal, you will notice improved customer care, higher employee engagement, increased revenue, and lower overall costs.

And a discipleship culture is both pervasive and contextual. It isn't something a leader "adds" to the organization. It happens in many ways and on an ongoing basis. For example, you will notice discipleship in the form of employee modeling, formal coaching, Socratic questioning, oral feedback, written feedback, team assessments, formal training, customer feedback, project feedback, etc. And depending on the task or context, these things happen both vertically *and* horizontally.

Discipleship doesn't just happen over a cup of coffee or on a jog. Rather, discipleship happens at the crossroads of a team and a project, in real life, with real choices that lead to real consequences. Discipleship opportunities surround us:

- How we choose to work with a difficult boss communicates what we value.
- The way we engage the disengaged team member speaks to the leadership style we want replicated.
- What we choose to expense to the company speaks to how we manage other people's money.
- Making time for our spouses and kids communicates whether family is a priority for those who work with us.
- How we choose to encourage and critique the work of our teammates speaks to how we value people.
- The way we ask questions and listen tells others if we want a "speak first" or "listen first" culture.

When we follow Jesus's example, hearts and lives change, and changed people change everything around them.

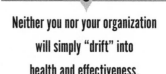

Neither you nor your organization will simply "drift" into health and effectiveness.

Think about how Jesus influenced His disciples. Instead of going to the synagogue and teaching a class every day for three years, He lived life with them. Discipleship happened at the intersection of daily events and consistently being together. They spent years traveling to towns and cities, speaking with religious and political leaders, sharing meals, visiting sick people, and having down time.

It's been said that we can impress from a distance, but only truly impact up close. That was the model Jesus used with His disciples—and God has since used His disciples to literally transform the world.

Fundamentally, mentorship is *serving* someone else in order to grow them, and discipleship is *submitting* yourself to something or someone. And make no mistake: we *all* submit to something or someone.

If someone wants to lose weight, good intentions alone won't get them there. They need disciplines and intentionality.

Similarly, neutrality and leadership are incompatible. Neither you nor your organization will simply "drift" into health and effectiveness. That's why anytime you are faced with a decision *for* or *against* God's way, discipleship happens. And the right choice leads to flourishing.

Discussion Questions:

1. Do you have a mentor? If not, why not?

2. Do you have someone you mentor? If not, why not?

3. If it is true that we cannot impart what we do not possess, what do you need to "possess" more from Him?

4. Have you ever thought about your organization as a primary site for discipleship? What does that mean to you?

5. Jesus and a small group of followers literally changed human history. Does it surprise you that such a massive impact began with so few people?

"And what you have heard from me in the presence of many witnesses entrust to faithful men, who will be able to teach others also." (2 Tim. 2:2)

"So, being affectionately desirous of you, we were ready
to share with you not only the gospel of God
but also our own selves, because you had become
very dear to us." (1 Thess. 2:8)

Chapter Nine

THE JOURNEY CONTINUES

The Road of Significance

"Father, make of me a crisis man. Bring those I contact to decision. Make me not a milepost, but a fork."

Those are the words of Jim Elliot, an American missionary who was murdered in the remote jungles of Ecuador while sharing the gospel with the Acua tribe. Although his life was cut short, it has had an impact far beyond what he could have imagined. Countless people have been inspired by his courageous faith to change the course of their lives. Even more incredibly, because of Elliot's example, and the continuing example of his wife, Elisabeth, many members of the Acua tribe began to follow Jesus. Elliot's life was like a stone dropped into a pond, and to this day the ripples of his influence continue to expand.

Crossroads force us to make decisions, and those decisions determine the influence we will have.

That is the role of a transformational leader: to bring people to a crossroad or decision point.

Crossroads force us to make decisions, and those decisions determine the influence we will have. In one direction we find selfishness and stagnation. The other brings health and love. God's way always directs our journey toward a deeper and more meaningful relationship with Him and others, which in turn yields greater influence on the lives around us.

If you are still reading at this point, you have a desire to do things most leaders won't do. Biblical leadership is not easy. God's ways are not easy. However, God always rewards the faithful, even if we don't see the evidence in this life.

Take a moment to reflect on this question:

- Have I ever made a decision to follow God's way and later regretted it?

It's impossible for us to imagine looking back at a decision to trust God and saying, "I really wish I *hadn't* trusted God— it would have been much better for me!" If you embrace a biblical view of leadership it will be harder and require trusting God more and yourself less. But it *will* change the quality of your relationship with God and those you influence.

Recall the practical scriptural truths that inform healthy leadership.

- True leadership begins with self-leadership.
- Effective conflict resolution transforms the workplace.
- Fear limits our impact, while God's perfect love casts out fear.
- Highly functional relationships at work change the culture.

- Leaders who fight for unity produce enormous positive momentum.
- Generous leaders are rare, refreshing, and deliver excellent ROI.
- The ultimate benefit of generous mentorship is a culture of discipleship.

A faithful and abiding relationship with Christ is the key that unlocks the door to this kind of healthy leadership. These are biblical principles, not tips to "try out." Even though it is true that you can apply these principles without a Christ-centered relationship, you will be operating from your own strength, so the long-term fruit won't be there. Your relationship with Christ is everything. We are designed to live and lead with God's love pouring into us, and as a result, His love also overflows into the lives of others.

The healthiest leaders and organizations *consistently demonstrate these behaviors.* God is the one calling you to be the greatest leader you can be. Don't miss out on the chance to participate in the work He has already prepared in advance for you to do.[63] And know that if God calls you, He *will* equip you. And in your obedience, you will discover the spiritually abundant life Jesus promised and unfathomable rewards in His coming kingdom.

The Truth About Greatness

"Who do you admire?"

Over the years, we've received quite a few answers to that question, covering everyone from Steve Jobs to Jesus.

"*Why* do you admire that person?"

---

63 Eph. 2:10.

People often hem and haw, as if their admiration was intuitive and never fully thought out. Eventually, however, everyone settles on a similar answer.

"Because they're great at what they *do*."

Few people will listen to or follow you unless you're credible. And two things give credibility: competence and character. Competence is being excellent at your work. A big piece of the puzzle when building a discipleship culture is hiring and developing people that *other* people will want to emulate. Great role models are central to building something that has enduring greatness.

Just as we initially admire people because of their competence at what they *do*, our admiration *deepens* because of who they *are*, as we watch their character in action.

Consider the NFL. There are many players who are objectively great at what they do. These are the best football players in the world. Yet why don't we admire them equally? If you are a parent, there are NFL quarterbacks you'd probably love for your son to emulate—just as there are quarterbacks you'd want to steer him away from!

As we saw earlier in Mark 10, two disciples ask Jesus if they can be the greatest in the kingdom of heaven—and fascinatingly, Jesus doesn't tell them no. Instead, He redefines how they think about greatness. The disciple's idea of being great focused on positional authority. One asked to sit at Jesus's left hand and the other at his right in the kingdom of heaven. Jesus helped them understand greatness is more directly related to sacrifice and service. To be truly great they needed to follow His example, both in service and suffering.

Do you want to be great? Praise God! Great leadership is the answer to most of our world's problems.

But are you willing to allow *God* to define your greatness?

Yes or no: are you willing to do whatever God asks of you, consistent with biblical values and your purpose, to fulfill the mission He may put in front of you?

This is a tough question. You might need to allow it to sink in for a moment before you answer it with honesty.

Not everyone answers yes. But those who do say yes discover that it is absolutely worth it.

If you choose to answer yes, you and many others will be eternally grateful for the way you followed Christ. However, no small sacrifice will be required from you.

And if you answer no, you must face the brutal fact that you are choosing to lead a relatively uneventful life, sacrificing eternal rewards for temporary comfort.

God wants more for you than comfort, but the decision is up to you.

The Road to Greatness

The surprising reality is we can achieve superior results in many of the areas we've discussed in this book, *and yet still miss our greatest opportunity as leaders.*

Practicing self-leadership, excelling at conflict resolution, building genuine relationships, fostering unity, and giving generously are excellent outcomes, but without love the results will lack eternal impact. Only what is done in love will last. As Proverbs 16:2 reminds us, "All the ways of a man are pure in his own eyes, but the LORD weighs the spirit."

God is calling leaders to something greater than achieving positive results for their organizations, as necessary and valuable as that is. At the heart of all we do, God is calling us to practice biblical love.

In one of the most impactful passages of the Bible, 1 Corinthians 13, we learn the characteristics of "love the verb."

According to God, love:

> is patient
> is kind
> does not envy
> does not boast
> is not proud
> does not dishonor others
> is not self-seeking
> is not easily angered
> keeps no record of wrongs
> does not delight in evil
> rejoices with the truth
> always protects
> always trusts
> always hopes
> always perseveres
> never fails

The chapter ends by declaring that love is the "greatest" virtue.

That isn't all the Bible says about love. First John 4 is a powerful passage that shows how love works in and through relationships, whether between God and His children or between humans.

> Beloved, let us love one another, for love is from
> God, and whoever loves has been born of God
> and knows God. Anyone who does not love does
> not know God, because God is love. In this the
> love of God was made manifest among us, that
> God sent his only Son into the world, so that

we might live through him. In this is love, not
that we have loved God but that he loved us and
sent his Son to be the propitiation for our sins.
Beloved, if God so loved us, we also ought to
love one another. No one has ever seen God; if
we love one another, God abides in us and his
love is perfected in us. ...

So we have come to know and to believe
the love that God has for us. God is love, and
whoever abides in love abides in God, and God
abides in him. By this is love perfected with us,
so that we may have confidence for the day of
judgment, because as he is so also are we in this
world. There is no fear in love, but perfect love
casts out fear. For fear has to do with punishment, and whoever fears has not been perfected
in love. (vv. 7–12, 16–18)

As we discussed in the previous section, fear can keep us
from truly following God. Fortunately, God's highest calling
for us, which is loving Him and others, is also the antidote
to fear. As God's love fills us, fear is pushed out. We gain the
boldness and faith to follow God wherever He is calling us.

Recall that when God gives us a *what*, He also gives us a
why. Love has very specific purposes. When Jesus was with
His disciples on the night before His crucifixion, He prayed
that they would understand and experience the perfect love
that is at the heart of His entire message. We read this in
John 17:20–26:

I do not ask for these only, but also for those who
will believe in me through their word, that they

may all be one, just as you, Father, are in me, and
I in you, that they also may be in us, so that the
world may believe that you have sent me. The glory
that you have given me I have given to them, that
they may be one even as we are one, I in them and
you in me, that they may become perfectly one,
so that the world may know that you sent me and
loved them even as you loved me. Father, I desire
that they also, whom you have given me, may be
with me where I am, to see my glory that you have
given me because you loved me before the foundation of the world. O righteous Father, even though
the world does not know you, I know you, and
these know that you have sent me. I made known
to them your name, and I will continue to make
it known, that the love with which you have loved
me may be in them, and I in them.

There is a necessary connection between unity, love, and
mission. Jesus says that *because* of our complete unity we will
demonstrate to the world something even more important
than unity: God's perfect love. Jesus wants us (His followers)
to experience the same unity and love that Jesus experiences
with His Father. When that happens, the world will know
two things: that Jesus is truly the Son of God, and that God
the Father loves the world.

Consider what leading your organization might look like
in light of our calling to live in complete unity and to love
one another.

When issues come up at work, do you want to be right?
Does your desire to win take priority over relationships? And
what happens if you don't "win"? Do you respond in anger, or

with passive-aggressive behavior? What happens when you don't get your way?

Whatever you are arguing about—what we like to call "the presenting issue"—it is never more important than the relationship. Division occurs because someone isn't getting what they want. Unity and love flourish when we decide the relationship will take priority over a specific issue we may need to work through over time.

You must decide *before* a disagreement occurs that leading God's way is more important than getting your own way. It takes more time to live this way and requires greater patience and understanding. Some disagreements take time to work through. That's okay. The relationships are worth it.

For example, when you decide your business partner's friendship is more important than getting your own way, you will approach conversations differently. You will no longer be looking for a way to get someone to *agree* with you, but rather for opportunities to love and serve your business partner. You will be motivated by questions such as:

- How can I understand his perspective?
- How can I make sure he knows how important he is to me?
- How can I keep an eternal perspective on this matter?
- How do I use this disagreement as a way to build a deeper friendship instead of letting it come between us?

These godly motives will drive you toward more complete unity and ultimately being a better expression of God's complete love, as we saw in John 17.

Further Along the Road

There is a danger that we will take the principles in this book and focus primarily on accomplishing goals, without considering *how* the goals are accomplished.

The opening verses from 1 Corinthians 13 are incredibly relevant for leaders. Before Paul defines love, as we read above, he offers a caution.

> If I speak in the tongues of men and of angels,
> but have not love, I am a noisy gong or a clang-
> ing cymbal. And if I have prophetic powers, and
> understand all mysteries and all knowledge, and
> if I have all faith, so as to remove mountains, but
> have not love, I am nothing. If I give away all I
> have, and if I deliver up my body to be burned,
> but have not love, I gain nothing. (vv. 1–3)

Thinking as humans, we would revere a person who does all these things, even without love. We might call that person a saint. But God's ways are not our ways. Even the best actions, when done without love, are incomplete.

When it comes to biblical love, embrace the idea of progress, not perfection.

Almost anyone can love someone who is lovable. What credit is that to them? The way we know we've moved toward kingdom building is when we are motivated by love toward all. In Matthew 5, Jesus prompts us to think differently about love, since godly love is for everyone.

> You have heard that it was said, "You shall love
> your neighbor and hate your enemy." But I say to

you, Love your enemies and pray for those who
persecute you, so that you may be sons of your
Father who is in heaven. For he makes his sun rise
on the evil and on the good, and sends rain on the
just and on the unjust. For if you love those who
love you, what reward do you have? Do not even
the tax collectors do the same? And if you greet
only your brothers, what more are you doing than
others? Do not even the Gentiles do the same?
You therefore must be perfect, as your heavenly
Father is perfect. (vv. 43–48)

And what does perfect mean? Filled with God's love—
exhibiting and acting on a biblical love for everyone, in every
situation. Clearly this isn't humanly possible, but hopefully
our lives begin to look more and more like this over time.
When it comes to biblical love, embrace the idea of progress,
not perfection.

Remember, God loved the world so much that He sent His
Son to die for us, *while we were still sinners.* When we were at
our worst, He loved us, and made the greatest sacrifice imaginable for us. We are to do the same for those who may be at their
worst in our lives. Why else would God, in His providence,
allow our paths to cross?

Leading with love is put to the test when you must deal
with someone who is unkind, angry, or hard to work with.
Those are the situations that require, and test, real love.

For instance, if you struggle with being patient, you
won't grow in that area when you spend time with someone
who doesn't require patience. But what if you are asked to be
patient with someone who is unbearable and may not even
deserve your patience? Now *that* will produce growth.

The same is true of the other elements of love: kindness, humility, forgiveness, and so on. Can you be kind to an unkind person? Can you be humble around a braggart? Can you forgive a spiteful person?

Colossians 3:14 speaks to this: "And above all these put on love, which binds everything together in perfect harmony." In *every* good thing you do as a leader, "put on love." Practice self-leadership with love, resolve conflict with love, and so on.

The amazing thing about the way God has designed us is this: when we practice biblical love, we will discover our affection *growing* for the unlovable. What begins as simple obedience, despite our feelings, can become friendship or even joy.

This happens when we keep active love as the focus of the relationship. Recall the story of Matt and Rob in chapter 3. At one point in their relationship they were more concerned with being right and getting their way than with loving each other. Each thought they had better, stronger ideas than the other. Ironically, it was only after they began to treat each other with biblical love that they discovered the true strength of their relationship. And their relationship has never been stronger.

Love in action is the ultimate witness. Whether in one-on-one relationships, within our organizations, or in our wider communities, love in action testifies to God's love in a deep and meaningful way.

Unconditional love is impossible unless we have personally experienced it. First John 4:19 puts it this way: "We love because he first loved us." Once we've experienced God's perfect love, and as we continue to abide in that love, we can pass that love on.

When we do, we'll be fulfilling our greatest opportunity and calling as leaders.

Read with Caution

This is both a leadership book and a theology book.

What we believe about God drives our behavior. What we believe about God determines how we lead.

Do you want to lead with love, service, and grace? That flows from your daily relationship with Christ.

The Bible tells us that we love because God first loved us. Understanding that God loves you right now—and will always love you—enables you to love. That means you choose to *act* with love. When you love, you are demonstrating the fruit of the Spirit. You choose to forgive someone when they wrong you. You choose to be kind when someone is ugly toward you. You choose to submit to the leading of the Spirit instead of the world.

This all flows from *God's active love*. John 3:16 says, "For God so loved the world..." You know what comes next. God *acted*. He took the initiative to send His Son, Jesus, in order to save us.

Bob Goff has a memorable phrase: *love does*. But active love must also strive to be effective. God doesn't take action for the sake of action, but for the sake of *accomplishing* His good purposes in our lives and in the world. "The impact God has planned for us does not occur when we're pursuing impact. It occurs when we're pursuing God."[64]

Unfortunately it is all too easy to act efficiently without being *effective*. Once Jeff was making world-record time driving to meet others from his office, when he received a call from his colleagues asking where he was. About the same time he looked up and saw the Louisiana state line! He had

---

64 Phil Vischer, quoted in Mark Batterson, *Primal: A Quest for the Lost Soul of Christianity* (Colorado Springs: Multnomah, 2010), 165.

been moving fast and making good time, but in the wrong direction—efficient but ineffective. We need to pray our character is molded by Christ into someone who can "be" *and* "do." Grace *and* excellence. Forgiveness *and* accountability.

A biblical example is the story of Jesus's visit to the village where His friends Mary and Martha lived. As Martha worked diligently, Mary sat at the feet of Jesus. When she asked Jesus to direct Mary to help, Jesus reminded Martha that what Mary was doing was better. The challenge for so many hard-charging leaders is to have the industriousness of Martha's hands, while also having the still and worshipful heart of Mary. We need both, and we need to model both with our teams. Action *with* purpose. Heart *with* impact. This is how Christ is calling us to lead.

This depends on God, 100 percent. There is a mystery in that, but we can trust God to accomplish His promise to complete His work in us in Christ even if we don't understand it.[65] Looking back, both of us are eternally grateful to God that we aren't the same people today that we were a decade ago. And by God's grace we won't be the same ten years from now. God is preparing us for eternity, just as He is preparing you.

God's mercies are new every morning, and His grace is entirely sufficient. God loves you, deeply and forever. Nothing will ever change that. That is the truth on which you now stand, looking ahead at the road God has set before you. There will be crossroads, but each wise decision you make will lead you closer to a God-honoring destination.

When a leader abides with Christ and models a discipleship culture, there is nothing to fear. Imagine the possibilities:

---

65 Phil. 1:6.

- What if you viewed your organization as a ministry and a mission field?
- What if you became more dependent on your relationship with Christ in your day-to-day business decisions?
- What if you had a band of brothers or sisters to talk through life's most difficult challenges, instead of making decisions alone?
- What if your church could more effectively equip and utilize entrepreneurs and business leaders?
- What if your employees grew as professionals and as people as a result of working with you?

Consider the impact on your employees. On your corporate culture, your clients, and your community.

Consider the impact on your personal walk with God and the resulting joy. You will be more thankful and filled with more grace. You will have more opportunities to serve Him. You will create better businesses, better churches, better families, and better cities.

God desires that these things happen. "For the eyes of the LORD run to and fro throughout the whole earth, to give strong support to those whose heart is blameless toward him" (2 Chron. 16:9).

All of this comes back to God's grace. You may have heard grace described as *God's Riches At Christ's Expense*. God has access to infinite *everything*. Power, knowledge, gifting, wisdom, forgiveness, creativity…the list goes on. And *we* have access to those riches in Christ, who freely gives us these gifts when we ask for them.[66]

---

66 James 1:5.

Unfortunately, we live in a world that glorifies the momentary. We see a five-second clip of an athlete who makes a catch requiring otherworldly reflexes and athleticism. A catch, in other words, we could never make, even after a thousand tries.

But that's exactly the point: *what the highlight doesn't show are the ten thousand practice catches the athlete made before the highlight.*

As you lead with excellence, it is essential to remember that God loves you, day in and day out. Through every up and down of life, God loves you. God doesn't demand or even expect perfect behavior. He doesn't want you to hide your failures. He knows you need Him, which is why He sent you His Son.

What God *does* ask is that you learn to obey and be faithful, in both big and small things, even when no one is watching. Do your best with every detail, no matter how insignificant it may seem. Why? Think of a carpenter who designs furniture that could last for generations...but just can't *quite* get the geometry right. Will he *ever* be regarded as a master of his craft? Just the opposite: he will likely be mocked for not having the required skills.

It works the same way spiritually. Be faithful in the small things, step by step, and you will be given more opportunity. Excellence honors God and inspires others. Habitual excellence, along with habitual honesty and grace, creates the context for discipleship. And discipleship is the mechanism by which people are truly changed.

The Journey Ahead

Healthy leaders have two goals.

The first is to lead your organization well today. God has given you stewardship responsibility for the sake of others. Like Jim Elliot, the way you choose to live and lead will make a tangible difference in many lives, including the lives of people you don't even know. That is a high calling.

The second goal is eternal, and it is directly related to your goal today. Everything you do at work has an eternal consequence. Jesus will dismiss the work that didn't matter. Everything we did with selfish motives will be discarded. However, all that we do for the glory of God and the benefit of others will last into eternity.

Jesus encourages us to stay focused on the eternal when He tells us to avoid storing up for ourselves treasures on earth, where they will be destroyed, and instead to store up treasures in heaven. We do that by investing in work that glorifies God and helps other people. Be great at your work for God's glory, and be faithful—because as you do, eternity will be that much more enjoyable, challenging, and fulfilling. The good things you experience in a great organization are a taste of unimaginably better things to come!

What do you love about leadership? Is it developing people and seeing them succeed? Creating new products that improve people's lives? Working to turn around struggling ventures? Whatever inspires you and honors God, be great at those things now, and eternity will be forever changed. Before sin entered the world, Adam and Eve were made to work, and they loved it. Before sin, work was not a punishment, but a privilege. Our role models on the pages of Scripture worked, as judges and kings and artists and doctors and generals. We are created by God to do good works with our talents, for the sake of others and for His glory.

Our eternal goal is this: to stand before God and hear Him say to us, "Well done, good and faithful servant. You have been faithful with a few things; I will put you in charge of many things. Come and share your master's happiness!"

For *eternity*.

Eternity will be infinitely more fulfilling than the most ful-filling thing you have ever experienced on earth. Perhaps we will have the privilege of telling God, "I can't believe you're letting me bless this many people in heaven. Thank you *so* much."

> It is only by *being* more that we can *do* more, first in our lives and then in our organizations. This is the road to greatness.

Have you heard the saying, "You're so heavenly minded you're no earthly good?" That expression is absolute nonsense. The more heavenly minded we are, the *more* earthly good we are.

You desire to make an impact, both now and in eternity. But you still must stand at the crossroads and choose this day whom you will serve.

We don't believe the invitation at this crossroad is merely to *do* more, but rather to *be* more. More connected to Christ, more dependent on His grace, more grateful for God's for-giveness and love, more vulnerable, more willing to fail, and more dependent on God in the face of fear. God doesn't *need* us to accomplish His will, but He chooses to invite our par-ticipation. As we submit to God, He will use us in amazing and satisfying ways.

It is only by *being* more that we can *do* more, first in our lives and then in our organizations. This is the road to greatness.

You can't change your company. You can't even funda-mentally change yourself.

But *God* can change *you*.

And leaders changed by God change the world.

Discussion Questions:

1. Can you truly say that you want something beyond comfort in this life?

2. As the Bible defines godly love, where do you need to grow the most?

3. Have you prioritized relationships at the expense of a traditional "business decision"? What was the result?

4. Does it sound strange to say that loving others is your highest calling as a leader?

5. Which possibilities of consistently abiding with Christ inspire you and give you the most hope?

6. Your work and leadership have eternal consequences. How does that perspective change the way you think and act each day?

No soldier gets entangled in civilian pursuits,
since his aim is to please the one who enlisted him.
An athlete is not crowned unless he competes
according to the rules. It is the hard-working farmer who
ought to have the first share of the crops.
Think over what I say, for the Lord will give you
understanding in everything. (2 Tim. 2:4–7)

Therefore, since we are surrounded by so great
a cloud of witnesses, let us also lay aside every weight,
and sin which clings so closely, and let us run with
endurance the race that is set before us,
looking to Jesus, the founder and perfecter of our faith,
who for the joy that was set before him endured the cross,
despising the shame, and is seated at the right hand
of the throne of God. (Heb. 12:1–2)

APPENDIX A

Leadership Skills Inventory

For each statement, please check the appropriate box.

Statement	Strongly Agree	Agree	Disagree	Strongly Disagree
1 Gives appreciation to others				
2 Confronts people with problems/situations as they arise				
3 Spends time "walking floor" and stays close to team member activity				
4 Gives encouragement to others				
5 Makes clear to individuals what is expected on the job				
6 Is a good listener				
7 Coaches/counsels employees to ensure compliance with goals				
8 Treats people with respect (i.e., like they are important people)				
9 Is actively involved in the development of those who report to him/her				
10 Holds people accountable for meeting the standards set				
11 Gives credit to those who deserve it				
12 Shows patience and self-control with others				
13 Is a leader people feel confident following				
14 Has the technical skills necessary to do the job				
15 Meets the legitimate needs (as opposed to wants) of others				
16 Is able to forgive mistakes and not hold grudges				
17 Is someone people can trust				
18 Does not engage in backstabbing others (e.g., talking behind backs, etc.)				
19 Gives positive feedback to team members when appropriate				
20 Does not embarrass people or punish them in front of others				
21 Sets high goals for self, team members, and department				
22 Has a positive attitude on the job				
23 Is sensitive to the implications of their decisions on other departments				
24 Is a fair and consistent leader and leads by example				
25 Is not an over-controlling or over-domineering person				

General Questions

1 What are the greatest leadership strengths/skills that the person being evaluated possess?

2 What leadership skills does the person being evaluated need to work on and improve?

Note: Survey adapted from *The World's Most Powerful Leadership Principle* by James C. Hunter

Matt's Acknowledgments

This book is the result of the collective wisdom of those who have invested in us. Hopefully the result is something helpful to others. I recognize we were the fortunate ones who received the "on the job" training, while the reader is receiving the written "training materials." Nonetheless, I'm grateful to acknowledge the leaders and teachers who have passed on their wisdom to me, many times at a moment when they were also providing care and correction to my previous incorrect ways of thinking.

Amy Levy, you are the most influential partner and friend I have. Your wisdom, counsel, and love are incredibly helpful. When I listen carefully to you, things tend to work out. When I don't, well—I should have! Thank you for being as patient, helpful, kind, and loving as you have been during this project.

Mom and Dad, thank you for the way you loved and sacrificed for our families over the years. I understand more now about how much you love us that we have our own kids. Nothing about this project would have been possible without your love, encouragement, and help. I love you too!

Jeff Ward and David Jacobsen, thank you for shaping, developing, writing, and iterating on this work. Your partnership in this project has made it far better than it would have been otherwise. You are diligent, thoughtful, and gifted leaders.

Rob Borrego, thank you for your patience, perseverance, and love through all of our highs and lows. Thank you for your friendship, partnership, and dedication to me and our company. You have made me into a better human. Only heaven knows what awaits from this work called Credera. I can't wait until we are able to see fully all that God has been up to.

David Dobat, Kyle Kaigler, and Kyle Thompson, thank

you for helping us figure things out. It only took 1,287 times, but eventually your biblical counsel took root and grew. It is hard to believe that friends like you exist, but you do. Every man needs men like you in his life.

Justin Bell, Scott Covington, Trent Sutton, Andrew Warden (alphabetically in case you are wondering), I love the friends you have become over the years. It is amazing to think back through all of your contributions and celebrate the leaders you are and how you have helped grow all of us into better leaders. Your thinking and influence is baked into this book by the way you have led and served others over the years here. I continue to watch, listen, and learn from you.

Credera employees, marketing, leadership, and partner teams. Your lives teach me in unexpected ways. It is encouraging when you provide a point of view not previously considered and challenge conventional ways of thinking. You make things better and you fight against entropy both inside Credera and with our clients. You are a markedly different and positive group. I look up to and respect you. You have provided the business sandbox to practically test humility, excellence, and integrity. You have no idea how encouraging it is, both personally and professionally, when I see you live those ideas out daily.

Those who contributed to the book's development process. We made significant changes to the book based on their recommendations, and we are very grateful for Morgan Eseke, Robert Alpert, John McGee, Ashley Sheetz, Rob Borrego, Andy Love, Aaron Graft, Kyle Thompson, Chuck Anderson, Benson Hines, Amy Levy, and Greg Crooks. And to Lauren King, special gratitude for helping guide this book through the publication process.

Todd Wagner and Joe White, you have set an example for how to live these leadership principles in real life. In my mind I see an image of you teaching or modeling the individual virtues discussed in this book. The educational value you have provided through your lives is a gift I will never be able to repay. Thank you for both your friendship and leadership.

Jeff's Acknowledgments

As I "gleaned the fields" of notes, anecdotes, principles, and stories during the writing of this book, I became even more aware of the profound influence of so many in my life and how their wisdom has impacted and influenced me even more than I realized. These are the "blessings" of friendships, family, mentors, and colleagues over the years.

Kristie Ward, you inspire, encourage, and motivate me daily. I am forever grateful for the ways in which you have modeled sacrificial service in our family and so many others. Faithful friend. Loving wife. Discipling mom. And now... writing partner!

Mom and Dad, you both gave me the gift of watching you faithfully proclaim the gospel in ministry and demonstrate the gospel in the lives of literally thousands of people. I have learned from you what it looks like to invest every gift and every ounce of energy and passion for eternal purposes.

Matt Levy, thank you for inviting me to participate in this project, and for the many years of watching you develop an amazing company, built on biblical principles. This book is a natural extension of the way you consistently seek to serve others, and help them take their next step toward faithfulness.

David Jacobsen, I can't even begin to thank you for the ways you helped to make not just the finished work, but the process of writing this book such a joy. It is evident that your faith informs your writing and I am so thankful for your ability to take volumes of thought and words (we don't lack for words!) and help bring shape, structure, and clarity.

My law partner and friend George Boll, thank you for your encouragement, integrity, model of care for staff, and excellence with people as well as the practice of law.

My External Focus Team at Watermark Community Church, thank you for your patience with this flawed leader and the ways in which you have shaped me and helped make our team one in which it is a joy to be "on mission" together as we serve the body and our city.

Todd Wagner and our Watermark Elders, your friendship, leadership, encouragement, giftedness, and service have blessed me beyond measure. So many of these principles are "caught" rather than "taught" and I have caught most of them from you.

Author Bios

Matt Levy is cofounder and managing director of Credera, a management consulting, user experience, and technology solutions firm based in Texas. Credera is the sandbox where most of the ideas discussed in this book have been learned and practiced over the last 20 years. Credera has been recognized by several notable organizations including Fortune's 100 Best Medium Workplaces, Fortune's Best Workplaces for Millennials, Inc. 5000's Fastest Growing Private Companies, Texas Monthly's Best Companies to Work for in Texas, Houston Business Journal Best Places to Work, and Dallas Morning News' Top 100 Places to Work. Learning to practice The Business of Faith has turned out to be one of the most challenging and rewarding experiences of Matt's career. Matt and his wife, Amy have two teenagers in Dallas and are members of Watermark Community Church. Matt can be reached on Twitter @mattOlevy

Jeff Ward was a trial lawyer in Dallas for many years, specializing in products liability litigation. He expanded his practice and joined some partners to create their own firm in 2002, handling complex products liability and commercial litigation. Jeff was named a "Texas Rising Star" by the publishers of Texas Monthly and served for many years as an adjunct professor. In 2008, he joined the staff of Watermark Community Church, where he has served as the Director of External Focus. He leads the church's international and local community engagement strategies, particularly in the areas of poverty, justice, education, and families/health and enjoys coaching kingdom-minded entrepreneurs who wish to use their gifts, skills, and passions in community transformation initiatives. He lives in Dallas with his wife and two sons. Jeff can be reached on Twitter @Jeff_R_Ward

Writer Bio

D. R. Jacobsen believes "that the story of any one of us is in some measure the story of us all," a conviction that shapes his collaborative writing and editing—and a phrase of Frederick Buechner's that he's fond of stealing. He holds a BA in English from Westmont College, an MA in theology from Regent College, and an MFA in creative writing from Seattle Pacific University. As David Jacobsen, his essays have appeared in various journals and anthologies, and he is the author of *Rookie Dad: Thoughts on First-Time Fatherhood*. As a collaborative writer he is represented by Don Jacobson of DC Jacobson & Associates. He and his wife have lived in California, Austria, and British Columbia, and now they make their home with their two boys in central Oregon. When not thinking about words, he plays pickup soccer, roots for the Timbers, and writes compelling bios. You can connect with him at jacobsenwriting.com.